The Air Force Plans for Peace, 1943–1945

THE AIR FORCE
PLANS FOR PEACE
1943–1945

Perry McCoy Smith

The Johns Hopkins Press
Baltimore and London

To Connor
in loving thanks
for accepting my goals as hers

Contents

Acknowledgments

The debts owed to many individuals can only be acknowledged; they can never be repaid. First, acknowledgment must go to those who were participants during this extremely exciting, busy, two-and-a-half-year period (1943–45) and who generously gave their time to answer what were often quite pointed questions. If the kindness showed by these persons is reciprocated by criticism in this book of their wartime actions, it is done so in the interest of scholarship and in the hope that a faithful rendition of the facts will be more useful than a glossing over of mistakes, inconsistencies, and misjudgments made under the burden of overwork and in the heat of war.

A special debt is owed to Miss Marguerite Kennedy, Chief Air Force Archivist, whose helpfulness and good cheer have to be experienced to be believed. Master Sergeant John S. Valdes, Jr., Mrs. Bea M. Estep, and numerous others on the staff at the Air University were most helpful. A great intellectual debt is owed Professor Warner R. Schilling, who helped me to select this topic and to formulate the questions to be asked, and who guided the research through its many vagaries.

To Colonel Wesley W. Posvar, who granted me time to complete the writing of this study, and to the instructors in the Department of Political Science, United States Air Force Academy, who shouldered my teaching load while I devoted myself to full-time research, a considerable debt is acknowledged.

Dr. Alfred Sears, Dr. William Coker, and Mr. Kit C. Carter, fellow researchers at the Air Force Archives, provided assistance by calling attention to documents which were often quite useful. Major Richard P. Dowell, who worked with me on the final portions of the editing and who devoted time while we were both engaged in combat flying during the Vietnam conflict, was most helpful.

I greatly appreciated the support and encouragement I received from Colonel Richard F. Rosser and Major Claude J. Johns, Jr., especially during my year in Thailand. Major Johns was particularly helpful during the final editing phases.

Mrs. Mary H. Bullock is largely responsible for the finished first draft of this book; she completed it under a serious time limitation. Connor D. Smith, as a competent typist, a meticulous editor, and, most of all, an understanding wife, contributed immeasurably to this book. The findings and conclusions are, of course, mine alone; they are not to be construed as carrying any official sanction of the Department of the Air Force or the Department of Defense.

Research and Terminology Note

The bulk of the research into primary materials was accomplished at the Air Force Archives at Maxwell Air Force Base, Alabama. The numbers used to identify documents apply to a double accounting system established within these archives. The first number is the more useful, since the majority of the documents can be located with it; I have added the second number because of the possibility that the archives may be reordered according to this second numbering system. When two sets of numbers are not listed, it is because the documents are not identified in the archives by both systems.

Any number that is preceded by the letters TS indicates that the document was originally top secret and remains filed in the top secret safes in the archives. All the documents referred to in this study have been downgraded to unclassified in accordance with Department of Defense directive 5200.9, but these unclassified documents remain filed with other documents that have not been downgraded. Any number that is preceded by the letters DAR indicates that the document comes from the daily activity reports of either of the two major planning groups within the staff of the Army Air Force, the Assistant Chief of Air Staff, Plans, or the Special Projects Office. These daily activity reports are useful in determining action taken which did not always become part of the official office files (meetings, telephone conversations, verbal orders, and discussions).

The Kuter Papers, located in the Special Collections Office of the United States Air Force Academy Library, were a useful source. The material is organized in two ways: large, bound books into which are pasted both personal and official data, and boxes which contain official records. The books are arranged chronologically and are organized into volumes and parts; the boxes are arranged chronologically by year. Reference to this material is made by indicating volume and part number or by indicating the year of the box.

Military abbreviations which are not in common usage are avoided in this study in order to eliminate the vexing problem of constant reference to a glossary. An exception is made to this rule when I refer to the three major planning offices: Assistant Chief of Air Staff, Plans (called the Air Staff, Plans), the Post War Division (called PWD), and the Special Projects Office (called SPO). Numerous references to these offices in certain chapters made abbreviation convenient. AC/AS-1 was Personnel; AC/AS-2 was Intelligence; AC/AS-3 was Operations, Commitments, and Requirements; AC/AS-4 was Materiel, Maintenance, and Distribution; AC/AS-5 was Plans. Since these abbreviations are awkward, the terms Air Staff, Personnel; Air Staff, Intelligence; Air Staff, Operations, Requirements and Commitments; Air Staff, Materiel; and Air Staff, Plans, will be used throughout. The Post War Division was a division of the major staff agency, the Air Staff, Plans. The Special Projects Office was separate from the Air Staff, Plans, and reported directly to General Arnold.

A short glossary to explain the abbreviations that are used has been included at the end of the book. Certain military terms may require a brief explanation that would be awkward in a glossary. "Aircraft," for example, is both singular and plural; the context and the grammar should be helpful in determining the number in each case. During the war the military used a system of indicating dates by placing the day, the month, and the year in that order. This system will be used throughout this book to avoid inconsistencies in usage between the text and any quoted material.

The word "tactical" causes particular difficulties, for the meaning of that word within the military has undergone an interesting evolution. Today, when referring to military action involving combat aircraft, "tactical" usually means any military action that is not strategic; in World War I it meant any military action; in World War II, the Army Air Force sometimes used "tactical" to mean a military action that was not strategic and sometimes used it to mean any military action. In this study the word will have its modern meaning, that is, tactical as opposed to strategic. Tactical aviation will be considered to be aviation involved in close support of ground troops (by delivering air ordnance on enemy targets within close proximity to the friendly front lines), interdiction of supply lines leading from the industrial rear areas to the front lines, and offensive air-to-air combat against enemy aircraft. Strategic aviation will be used to describe bombardment aviation whose primary purpose is to bomb targets within the enemy's heartland and which engages in air-to-air combat, if at all, strictly on a defensive basis.

Since numerous plans and outlines were written during the war which were intended for use in the postwar period or for use in the wartime period for postwar planning purposes, there is some problem in differentiating among them. The title of the plan will be used in this book, except that the three plans referred to most frequently—the Initial Post War Plan (105 groups), Post War Plan No. 2 (75 groups), and the 70-group plan (no title)—will normally be referred to by numbers of groups rather than by title.

The term "postwar" was sometimes spelled as one word, sometimes as two, and often was hyphenated by the postwar planners and Army Air Force leaders. I use the one-word spelling except in quoted material where spelling follows the quoted document.

Military rank causes some difficulty, since during the 1943–45 period there were many promotions among the Army Air Force leaders and planners. The rank used here will be that held by the particular individual at the time of the war when he is introduced. Officers referred to on numerous occasions will be initially introduced with their rank, and in subsequent references will usually be cited by the last name only.

There was a tendency on the part of many officers within the military to emphasize points in plans and correspondence by underlining key words or phrases. To avoid frequent discussion in the footnotes of the source of the underlining, I have refrained from adding any myself; thus underlining within quoted material is that of the original author.

One section of the Air Staff which was deeply involved in planning during the war but was not a specified planning section was the Advisory Council, a personal staff to General Henry H. Arnold, Commanding General, Army Air Force. Members of this Council included Colonel Charles Pearre Cabell, Colonel Emmett O'Donnell, Jr., Colonel Jacob E. Smart, and Colonel Fred M. Dean. In addition, Arnold used his Deputy Assistant Chiefs of Staff much the same way he used his Advisory Council, as expediters and troubleshooters. Officers who held the position of Deputy Assistant Chief of Staff included Brigadier General Frederick H. Smith, Jr., Brigadier General Patrick W. Timberlake, and Brigadier General Hoyt S. Vandenberg. All of these men were very close to the decision-making process within the Army Air Force.

Introduction

In the course of human history certain dates have particular significance. The year 1945 is significant as both a commencement and a conclusion. This date marked the termination of the second great war of the century (or the end of a thirty years' war, depending on the perspective taken), the successful explosion of an atomic weapon, the reordering of the power structure among the states, and the long-delayed awakening of the aloof giant, the United States, from its increasingly fitful slumber behind the protective oceans and the arctic wastelands of Alaska, Northern Canada, and Greenland.

World War II followed on from many of the issues and with some of the weapons of World War I, but by 1945 there had been such transformations in the character of military technology, the distribution of power on this planet, and the foreign policy of the United States that world politics became significantly different thereafter. These transformations are probably clearer with hindsight than they were at the time, but observers during that period were at least partially aware of both the rapidity and the magnitude of change in the world arena.[1]

Before World War II the American military establishment was a small professional force of almost negligible political significance, either domestically or internationally, except in time of war and in the immediate postwar periods. In the years covered by this study it became an enormously important political and economic influence, domestically and internationally, in time of peace and in time of war. I have attempted to show how one branch of the military, the Air Force, perceived and prepared for this great transformation.

The focus of the work is on the planning of the U.S. Army Air Force during the war with regard to military aviation policy in the postwar world. It is a case study of the methods and processes of military planning. By concentrating on a specific group of planners, on what influenced them, and on how accurate they were in their perceptions and predictions, we can see precisely the kinds of problems, pitfalls, and blindspots that were experienced by U.S. military planners in their first systematic attempt to anticipate the future. The lessons to be learned have current as well as historical interest. It takes no particular acumen to note that since World War II the military has had a significant role in the formulation of U.S. foreign policy. It therefore behooves us to know as much as possible about how it operates.

1. For a perceptive 1944 study of this topic, see William T. R. Fox, *The Superpowers: The United States, Britain, and the Soviet Union—Their Responsibility for Peace* (New York: Harcourt, 1944).

I

I can indicate the scope of my work by recording the major questions I sought to answer. They are: What led the Army Air Force to engage in long-range planning? How does a long-range planning section remove itself in wartime from operational problems and concentrate on long-term objectives? What was it hoped that the Air Force would achieve in the postwar period? What implicit and explicit theories of international relations did the planners hold? How did they view the role of international organizations? What role in their thinking was played by personal ambitions and interservice rivalry? How much were they motivated by the necessity to compete with the other branches of the military for the postwar budget? Did they feel threatened by the prospect of industry turning from military to civilian production? And, perhaps most important, did the planners accurately foresee the postwar threats to this nation? Was the planning successful?

The period of investigation, 1943–45, was chosen because it provides more insights into military planning for international contingencies by the U.S. military than any other period in modern times. The decision-making power of United States military leaders was then greater than it ever had been before and perhaps greater than it has been since 1945. With the Secretaries of War and Navy and the Department of State largely removed from the decision-making process, especially in the last two years of the war, the American military leaders were making military and political decisions unaided for the most part by civilian agencies or advisors.

Nineteen forty-three is a somewhat arbitrary date. The logical place to begin would be the commencement of postwar planning. But this date is difficult to pinpoint, since most planning during the war itself (assuming the war started for the United States on 7 December 1941) had some postwar considerations either explicitly or implicitly involved. In fact, there is evidence that some planning for postwar contingencies was subtly integrated into such prewar plans for the conduct of the impending war as "Munitions Requirements of the Army Air Forces to Defeat our Potential Enemies," drawn up in August 1941. This important plan incorporated the doctrine of supremacy of strategic airpower over other forms of military aviation; it was intended to order doctrinal and procurement priorities before, during, and after the impending war.[2]

In 1943, offices and organizations were established both within the War Department and within the Army Air Force that were given the specific tasks of postwar and demobilization planning. The first studies of postwar requirements were written in 1943, though the first formal plan for the initial postwar Air Force was not completed until February 1944.

Nineteen forty-five was selected as the cutoff date for several reasons. First, I wanted to limit my investigation to wartime planning as such. The rapid demobilization which undermined the effectiveness of the

2. Document AWPD/1. 145.82–1.

United States forces did not begin in earnest until 1946; until January of that year the United States was still on a wartime economic footing, reconversion of factories to peacetime production had not yet taken place, and the majority of American forces and equipment were still deployed overseas. Second, this cutoff enables us to see more clearly the perceptiveness of the Air Force planners, for as of 1 January 1946 the future difficulties with the Soviet Union were largely unperceived by the general public, military and naval planners, or the State Department. Thus, any assumptions as to future enemies made by the AAF planners prior to that date were not based on the self-evident threat from the Soviet Union which was to come in 1946.[3] Third, after 1 January 1946 the leadership in the War Department and within the Army Air Force had changed appreciably, because by then Marshall, Stimson, and Arnold had all passed from the scene. Finally, although this study could end on V-J Day or on the day Japan sued for peace, the selection of either of these dates would largely eliminate a period of considerable interest, especially in relation to the atomic bomb and the weapon's impact on postwar planning.

Although the data available were sufficient for me to answer my major questions adequately, several remarks about the limitations of the study are in order. Because it is extremely hazardous to separate what is unique in this case from what may be typical and repetitive in military plans, some of my generalizations should be considered as tentative. Two other problems have to do with the sources. First, some of the data came from interviews, and I encountered the usual difficulties when the participants were asked to recall specific events. Although the interviewees struggled admirably with their memories, attitudinal changes over the past twenty years were sometimes difficult to ignore completely. With a very few exceptions, they showed uncommon objectivity and answered most, though not all, of the questions that the written record left unanswered. Second, I was unable to gain access to the records of the Joint Chiefs of Staff. Although this study is concerned with the Army Air Force postwar planning, access to the Joint Chiefs of Staff and Combined Chiefs of Staff material would have been helpful in determining more exactly the flow of ideas and the circumstances of decision-making. In some cases, tentative statements must be made, where access to JCS records might have permitted greater certainty. Fortunately, most of the AAF plans and numerous memoranda in the planning files, which periodically summed up the progress of postwar planning, refer specifically to external directives received from the War Department, JCS, the State Department, and the President, strategic assumptions made by the War Department or the JCS, and specific planning guidance obtained from sources outside the Army Air Force. Since

3. Churchill's Fulton, Missouri, speech of March 1946 is as useful as any point to identify the beginning of general American awareness of the Soviet danger. Identification of the Soviet Union as a potential enemy was, in fact, made as early as 1944, but the rationale for it was not the result of any overt, hostile act by the Soviet Union.

many of the official JCS documents of the wartime period were found in the Arnold Papers and in the Air Force Archives, and since the Chief Air Force Archivist is quite sure that the Air Force Archives contain either the original wartime files or reproductions of the files of all the staff agencies within the Army Air Force, the nonaccess to JCS files was not a crucial limitation. In fact, none of these limitations, in any significant way, diminishes the potential utility of this study.

The Organization of the Planning Function and the Qualifications of the Planners

The importance of the January 1943 Casablanca Conference as it affected Army Air Force planning was considerable. It was at this conference that General Henry H. Arnold realized that AAF planning as he had originally conceived it was much too narrow. Arnold's initial conception of the Air Staff, Plans, was an operational planning section that would chart the next campaign, search for new weapons systems, and give some guidance to the AAF in establishing its goals and in indicating how to reach them.

Casablanca was a rather traumatic experience for all the United States military planners who attended; they came suddenly to the realization that the British military were much better prepared than they.[1] On 27 April 1943, Colonel J. E. Smart of Arnold's Advisory Council recommended in a memorandum to Arnold that prior to

. . . the next Casablanca conference [I] recommend you point out:

a. That the U.S. Chiefs of Staff must agree among themselves as to the course of action that must be followed by the United Nations,

b. That presidential approval of this course of action be obtained prior to meeting with the British,

c. That the United States Chiefs of Staff force the British to implement the plan of action agreed upon by the United States Chiefs of Staff and the President.[2]

Casablanca brought home to the AAF leaders the importance of detailed planning, the need for coordination and agreement between interested departments and agencies prior to any confrontation with allied representatives, and the need to integrate political considerations with military strategic planning. The necessity for planning in the technological area had long been appreciated; but now for the first time the Air Staff, Plans, was able to generate long-range plans that would consider political as well as military and technological factors, and to do so with some hope that Generals Arnold and Marshall would give time and thought to them and not regard political considerations as completely irrelevant and outside the purview of the American military.

The experience of the Air Staff at Casablanca was not the only reason for the establishment of the two offices—the Special Projects Office and the Post War Division of the Air Staff, Plans—which were to undertake the planning for the postwar world. By the summer of 1943 there had been a number of queries from the State Department, as well

---

1. In the words of General Wedemeyer, "We came, we listened, and we were conquered." Albert C. Wedemeyer, *Wedemeyer Reports* (New York: Henry Holt, 1958), p. 192.
    2. 145.81–80.

as from many wartime agencies, requesting AAF ideas on postwar requirements. As the AAF was organized in 1943, there was no office specifically designed to handle these queries, and Arnold decided to establish one, separate from his major staff offices, to sift through these queries and to coordinate the various actions required during the immediate post-hostilities period. The Special Projects Office was established by Arnold in April 1943 to coordinate the postwar planning of the Army Air Force with that of the War Department, as well as with the plans of the many executive agencies concerned with demobilization, reconversion of industry, disposal of surplus goods, retraining of service personnel, and other postwar problems.[3]

Another important event in the planning area, not directly related to the lessons of Casablanca or to the incessant requests for Army Air Force postwar plans, was the return of Brigadier General Laurence S. Kuter from his combat assignment in Tunisia (where he had served as the Deputy Commander for the Northwest African Tactical Air Force) to become the Assistant Chief of the Air Staff, Plans.[4] Kuter quickly saw the need for a postwar planning section and, with the concurrence of Arnold (despite the possibility of overlap with the Special Projects Office), he formed the fourth division within Plans, the Post War Division, in the summer of 1943. The other divisions were the Joint Staff Division, the Logistics Division, and the Strategy Division.[5]

The War Department and the Army Air Force headquarters both underwent a number of major and minor organizational changes during the war that affected their planning. The creation of this Post War Division was the most significant change. Although postwar planning within the AAF was in progress before the creation of a specific division to handle it, previously the demands for wartime operational, logistical, and technological planning had precluded anything but an occasional cursory answer to questions relating to the postwar period.

By the summer of 1943, then, the Army Air Force had two offices which were given the primary task of postwar planning: the Post War Division of the major staff agency, the Air Staff, Plans, and the Special Projects Office, an office divorced from the five major staff agencies and reporting directly to General Arnold. In addition to the plans sections, each of the other major staff sections had a planning responsibility which related to the postwar world. Personnel, Intelligence, Operations, and Materiel all had requirements to be met in the post-hostilities period, but each of these sections deferred to the PWD for guidance on doctrine, force structures, and air bases in the postwar world. Any problem that required coordination with agencies outside the AAF was normally directed to the PWD and, in turn, to the SPO.

The key individuals in postwar planning were the Assistant Chief

3. Untitled Report of SPO, Tab D (September 1943), 1.126.81; 3457–4A.
4. Kuter Papers, 1943 box.
5. Directory Chart, Headquarters Army Air Forces (15 October 1943). 145.041A–21.

of Air Staff, Plans, the Chief of the Post War Division, and the Special Projects Officer. From 1943 to the termination of hostilities there was a remarkable degree of continuity in these three important positions. General Kuter was the Assistant Chief of Air Staff, Plans, from June 1943 until the spring of 1945. Major General Lauris Norstad was Kuter's replacement and served until the end of 1945. Brigadier General Pierpont Morgan Hamilton was briefly Chief of the Post War Division in the summer of 1943, but Colonel Reuben C. Moffat was Chief for the two crucial years from the autumn of 1943 to the end of 1945. Colonel F. Trubee Davison was the Special Projects Officer from the inception of the office until its elimination in September 1945.

Thus, in addition to Arnold, the key individuals in the area of post-war planning number only four. Since they all made large contributions to planning, a brief description of each might prove helpful.

Major General Kuter graduated from the United States Military Academy in 1927, forty-fourth in a class of 203. He was commissioned as a second lieutenant in the Field Artillery but after two years transferred to the Air Corps, in July 1929, and entered flying school.[6] By 1934 Kuter had become an exceptionally effective, intelligent, and hardworking young man who was selected to attend the Air Corps Tactical School at Maxwell AFB.[7] Most of Kuter's fellow students were captains and majors, while he was one of only 14 lieutenants in his class of 60.[8] Kuter, who graduated first in his class, established such an outstanding record that upon graduation he was chosen to remain as an instructor.[9]

During his tour of duty as instructor, Kuter formulated the concepts and habits that were to accelerate him to high positions of responsibility. A gifted lecturer, a conscientious researcher, and an inquiring scholar, he found that this position suited his abilities and inclinations superbly. The assignment had many frustrations, however, which led to the formulation of certain ideas that were to color his thinking in later years. These frustrations involved the unsuccessful attempt by Kuter and others to circulate the airpower concepts devised in the creative atmosphere of the Tactical School to the Army as a whole. Attempts to have articles on airpower published in service journals were often thwarted by U.S. Army Headquarters or by the editors of the journals.

This narrow, parochial attitude on the part of the other branches angered the logical young captain, who saw strategic airpower as the primary military arm of the future. The Coast Artillery Corps had the narrowest viewpoint in the 1930's, since the logic of coastal defense was being seriously questioned and Coast Artillery officers were trying desperately to defend an anachronism. In the summer of 1938 Kuter submitted an article entitled "The Bombardier Evaluates Antiaircraft

6. Kuter Papers, vol. I, p. 38.
7. *Ibid.*, vol. II, part I, p. 7.
8. *Ibid.*, p. 26.
9. Flint O. Dupre, ed., *U.S. Air Force Biographical Dictionary* (New York: Franklin Watts, 1965), p. 131.

Artillery" to the War Department General Staff, G-2 (Intelligence), which he hoped would be published in the *Coast Artillery Journal* on approval of G-2 and the editor of the journal. In his own handwriting Kuter indicated what resulted from this submission. "Cooly [*sic*] approved by G-2 if author deletes reference to inter-branch squabble (whole subject). Disapproved by G-2 because of criticism of tactics of branch other than author's.—Summer 1938." [10]

This narrow view whereby a military branch or service is intolerant of criticism from other services, is extremely protective of the missions its spokesmen feel are exclusively those of their service, and is unwilling to compromise with other services on roles and missions will subsequently be referred to as "parochialism."

Thus, in Kuter's formulative years, it was the conservative senior Army officers who thwarted his efforts. In reaction to the intransigence of these ground officers, Kuter and others on the faculty of the Tactical School turned to a kind of counterparochialism, which led to a doctrine of airpower that assigned a negligible role to the other services. This sincere belief in the ability of airpower to defeat any enemy through strategic bombardment, when added to the extreme parochialism of the older army branches, led the Tactical School, in general, and Kuter, in particular, to a theory of warfare that closely resembled the concepts of Giulio Douhet.

The influence of Douhet on the thinking of the Tactical School has long been debated. Recent evidence has been uncovered which rather conclusively proves that Douhet's *Command of the Air* was available in English at the Tactical School as early as 1923, that an air service manual on employment of air forces incorporated most of Douhet's ideas and terminology, and that the airpower theoreticians at the Tactical School in the late 1920's and 1930's relied heavily on his theories even though a number of these Air Corps instructors did not realize their intellectual debt to him. [11]

The doctrine developed by the officer faculty members of the Tactical School (Donald Wilson, Harold George, Kuter, and others) was similar to Douhet's, yet differed in at least one major area—target selection. Their concept was one of target selection based on the key vulnerabilities of a state's economy. Kuter polished the concepts propounded in the early- and mid-1930's, and when later called upon to develop operational plans he proved an extremely sophisticated and able proponent of strategic aviation, as well as a keen competitor whenever he encountered parochialism in the ground services. Kuter's viewpoint was certainly narrow itself, but it was based more on a reaction to Army parochialism than on any desire to deny the ground Army a role.

Most of the interviews for this book revealed that, of the men close to

10. 168.80–11; 2–8237–63.
11. Raymond R. Flugel, "United States Air Power Doctrine: A Study of the Influence of William Mitchell and Giulio Douhet at the Air Corps Tactical School, 1921–1935" (Ph.D. diss., University of Oklahoma, 1965), p. 201.

Arnold, Kuter must be considered the most brilliant and the most influential. Admiration for him, though almost universal among the participants, was not unqualified, for he was described as "extremely able, but personally ambitious" and an "empire builder." In my attempt to determine on whose counsel Arnold most heavily relied, I found that most of those interviewed responded immediately with Kuter's name, but quickly followed it with a qualification like that given above. There seemed to be a compelling need to evaluate Kuter, even though such an evaluation was not solicited. The interview with Kuter himself was most revealing, as it showed that he viewed the Army leaders as parochial, with the exception of Generals Marshall and Wedemeyer.

Perhaps all parochialism in the military is based on that perceived in others. There is no question that narrow-mindedness was widespread among ground officers in the 1930's and that Kuter's perception of it then was accurate. In the 1940's, however, his evaluation changed little, while in reality Army parochialism was slowly but definitely declining. The records show that despite the tendencies of certain Army officers, the Army generals demonstrated less parochialism during the war than did the Air Force or Navy officers.

General Kuter's wartime perspective was therefore inaccurate, and most top Air Force generals felt it unwise to antagonize Army leaders, since most were committed to Air Force autonomy. In large measure, Army parochialism was an illusion of Kuter—Arnold's closest advisor in Washington from 1943 to 1945. Kuter identified the wrong adversary, for it was the Navy that caused the Air Force its greatest postwar problems. This false identification led the Air Force to tilt at windmills, while the Navy was able to organize its forces effectively to battle the AAF on the question of unification.

By 1939, when General Marshall selected Kuter for a key planning post as a member of the Air Section of the G-3 Division of the War Department general staff, Kuter was equipped with all the professional and intellectual qualifications which would hurtle him past his contemporaries and many of his seniors in less than three years. By February 1942 he was the youngest general in the entire United States military and the only AAF general, with the exception of James Doolittle, who was promoted from lieutenant colonel to brigadier general without ever holding the rank of colonel.[12]

Kuter, more than anyone in the AAF, was responsible for the large amount of postwar planning that was done, but, unfortunately, it was influenced by his view of the Army. The departure of Kuter in the spring of 1945 and the arrival of General Norstad as the chief AAF planner changed postwar planning subtly but decisively, for Norstad, unlike Kuter, saw the Army leaders as allies in the drive for Air Force autonomy. Kuter's brilliance and farsightedness combined with Norstad's objectivity resulted in a great amount of planning for the

12. Kuter held the position of AC/AS, Plans, from 8 July 1943 to 8 May 1945. Kuter Papers, vol. V, part II, p. 20.

post-war world during the heat of the World War II operational decision making.

Major General Lauris Norstad graduated from the United States Military Academy 139th out of a class of 241 in 1930.[13] Norstad's only school assignment before the war began was at the Air Corps Tactical School, from which he graduated in December 1939.[14] He worked briefly in Washington from February to August 1942; as a member of the Advisory Council "he helped map the air offensive plans for World War II."[15]

Norstad spent most of the war in staff and planning positions in overseas theaters, returning to Washington to assume the position of Assistant Chief of Air Staff, Plans, in June 1945. The fundamental differences in background between Norstad and Kuter were the latter's instructor duty at Maxwell AFB in the 1930's and his long-time service in Washington immediately before and during the war.

The head of the Special Projects Office throughout its entire existence (April 1943 to September 1945) was Colonel (later Brigadier General) F. Trubee Davison. Davison, who was Assistant Secretary of War for Air from 1926 to 1933, had been asked by General Arnold in 1942 to return to government service to be Arnold's Special Assistant with the rank of colonel.[16] His academic background included B.A. and M.A. degrees from Yale University and an LL.B. from Columbia University. He was a naval aviator in World War I and had won the Navy Cross. He was also President of the American Museum of Natural History from 1933 to 1951.[17]

Colonel Reuben C. Moffat was head of the Post War Division from the autumn of 1943 until the end of 1945. After spending three years at Cornell University, from 1914 to 1917, he enlisted in the U.S. Army, became an aviator, and went to France in 1918. He was a graduate of the Air Corps Tactical School (1938) and Command and General Staff School at Fort Leavenworth, Kansas (1939).[18] As a result of an aircraft accident early in the war he was no longer on flying status nor available for combat duty. After a long convalescence he assumed the position of Chief of the Post War Division in the autumn of 1943. Trusted by Kuter for his good judgment and his longtime experience on the operational end of the Air Corps, Colonel Moffat strove manfully with a job that was initially difficult and, as the war drew to a close, increasingly

13. *Register of Graduates and Former Cadets of the United States Military Academy* (West Point, N.Y.: West Point Alumni Foundation, 1965), p. 412.

14. *Who's Who in Aviation: A Directory of Living Men and Women Who Have Contributed to the Growth of Aviation in the United States, 1942–1943* (New York: Ziff-Davis, 1942), p. 314.

15. Dupre, *Biographical Dictionary*, p. 179.

16. Interview with F. Trubee Davison, 30 April 1966.

17. *Who's Who in World Aviation* (Washington: American Aviation Publications, Inc., 1955), I, 76. Davison retained this position from 1942 to 1945 despite his wartime service.

18. Interview with Major General P. M. Hamilton, 14 July 1966.

demanding. The first chief of the division, Colonel P. M. Hamilton, had partially staffed this section and Moffat completed the job by late 1943. Some staff members were friends or acquaintances of the two men.[19] In general, these staff members had no operational experience in the AAF.[20] The Divison was not regarded as an attractive assignment, since it had nothing to do with the immediate war.[21]

The Special Projects Office had more capable officers and accomplished its part of the postwar planning mission with greater skill than did the Post War Division. However, the SPO was quite limited in what it could do for three reasons. Arnold had given Davison the task of coordinator and had specifically directed him not to usurp the planning function from the Air Staff, Plans; Davison, being in a rather difficult position considering his earlier experience as a high War Department official, was very cautious not to step beyond the guidelines that Arnold had laid down for him; and Davison's responsibility as the AAF Assistant to Army Major General William Tompkins, the Chief of the War Department's Special Planning Division, took up a great deal of his time.[22] The SPD was assigned the task of planning the demobilization of the Army at the end of the war, and as time passed, Davison's Special Projects Office became involved in that aspect of the postwar planning to the relative exclusion of other aspects.[23] Thus, to Colonel Moffat fell the full responsibility for postwar plans concerning the size and composition of forces, types of aircraft, and base requirements both within the United States and overseas. Kuter, and later Norstad, would make an occasional foray into this area, but the pressing operational planning demands of the war left these men little time for detailed inquiry into postwar planning.[24]

The United States military leaders had a certain distrust of the intellectual, the scholar, and the academician, largely as a result of the criticism directed at the military during the 1930's regarding its alleged joint responsibility with the "munition makers" for American involvement in World War I.[25] The military leadership, especially within the

19. *Ibid.*

20. Interview with Major General Haywood S. Hansell, 3 May 1966. Interview with Major General Norris B. Harbold, 28 June 1966. Interview with Brigadier General Sidney F. Giffin, 14 July 1966. General Hansell was on the faculty of the ACTS in the 1930's. General Harbold held important staff positions in the Training Command during the war. General Giffin was an Air Corps officer in the Operations Division of the War Department General Staff.

21. Interview with Lieutenant General Fred M. Dean, 12 May 1966. Interview with General Charles P. Cabell, 4 May 1966.

22. Davison interview.

23. Interview with Major General William F. Tompkins, 16 May 1966.

24. Interview with General Laurence S. Kuter, 19 May 1966. Interview with General Lauris Norstad, 25 May 1966.

25. Giffin interview. Cabell interview. Cabell expressed in his interview a concern that the anti-military bias of intellectuals was often reflected in their criticisms of the U.S. military. The distrust of intellectuals by high-ranking officers in the 1943–45 period and in more recent times seems to reflect less a basic anti-intellectualism than a serious questioning of the objectivity of the intellectuals who examine the military.

Army, felt that there was a direct relationship between this pre-World War II criticism and the inability of the military to obtain the funds necessary for a large force when the danger of war increased in the late 1930's.[26] Intellectuals within the military, however, were generally well regarded by General Marshall, who was largely responsible for establishing a planning group within the War Department's Operations Division (OPD) consisting of former Rhodes scholars and instructors from the Department of Economics, Government, and History at the United States Military Academy.[27] All these men had completed some graduate work in the social sciences, though none could be considered a qualified social scientist. Within the AAF itself there were no Rhodes scholars and only two instructors from this department at the Military Academy.[28] There were no professional Army or AAF officers who were also social scientists, and even the small group of military intellectuals who had some background in the social sciences was composed largely of Army rather than Army Air Force officers. General Arnold was a leader in calling upon civilian academic talent to assist him, but this group was made up of physical scientists and economists. Political scientists were not recruited by the Air Force, and, lacking any in-house expertise, it went without such talent in its planning. Norstad and Kuter were largely self-educated men in the sense that neither had been exposed to any formal graduate education, but they both spent much time in self-improvement through reading and study.

Arnold's ability to find competent people, even among junior officers with little operational experience within the AAF, was one of his finest talents (Colonel Fred M. Dean, class of 1938 at the Military Academy and a key member of Arnold's Advisory Council as a twenty-seven-year-old colonel, is an example). One thing these men lacked, for all their youth, vigor, and intelligence, was any previous contact with either the academic world or other branches of government.[29] Of all the officers on the planning staff, only one—Moffat—had attended the Army Command and Staff School. None had attended the War College or any graduate school. Although some had attended the Air Corps Tactical School at Maxwell AFB, this still had not brought them into contact with academe or government.

Despite the obvious limitations of individual members of the PWD, these men did spend their entire time on postwar planning. Thus, as the war drew to a close, two years of work by a dozen or so officers had been accomplished in the form of a number of alternative plans.[30]

26. *Ibid.*
27. Norstad interview.
28. Colonel S. F. Giffin and Colonel W. S. Stone.
29. Interview with General Jacob E. Smart, 16 May 1966. In Lieutenant General Ira Eaker's words: "I am certain that we do not have enough brain power on the planning side." Letter, Eaker to Arnold (11 July 1944), p. 1. 168.491; 3–4711–4.
30. The size of the Post War Division grew from eight officers in 1943 to twenty-two in late 1945.

The PWD had solicited ideas from the field and had coordinated through-out the Air Staff and the operational and training commands each completed plan, as a 1944 PWD memorandum illustrates:

> At various stages in planning it will be necessary to consult with other departments or agencies of this Headquarters, or to request assistance from subordinate commanders in the field. It is desired that the best thought and specialized knowledge available in the Air Forces will be represented in each completed portion of the Plan. Staff coordination by interested staff agencies will therefore be obtained before proceeding with each successive important phase.[31]

The operational commands generally presented ideas prior to plan formulation and commented upon each of the plans. The Post War Division evaluated these comments and incorporated into the plans what were felt to be useful ideas or criticisms. The men in postwar planning were not arrogant or stubborn; they accepted criticism well, and while they sought it only from operational military sources, largely neglecting technological and political considerations, the resultant plans were indicative of the type of up-to-date operational thinking common in the AAF.

The Post War Division remained separate from operational planning and did not get involved in the immediate wartime planning problems as might have been expected by certain students of the military bureaucracy.[32] There is no evidence that the PWD expended efforts on any other than the postwar planning period, with the exception of the time from victory in Europe (V-E Day) to the defeat of Japan (V-J Day). Since victory in Europe would mean redeployment, and since not all of the units to be returned to the United States were to be sent to the Pacific, the V-E to V-J period was closely connected with the post-V-J period.

With this one exception, the PWD limited its attention to the postwar period. Why did this division avoid the task of "putting out fires" within the Air Staff, Plans? There is reason to believe that four factors were paramount. First, the qualifications of the postwar planners were such that they lacked the kind of expertise which might have made them valuable as operational planners. None had had combat experience in World War II aircraft, most were not pilots, and few had had military experience prior to Pearl Harbor. The second factor was Colonel Moffat's unwillingness to take on assignments that did not relate directly to postwar planning. The third factor was that the

31. Memorandum for Lieutenant Colonel P. Shepley from Colonel R. C. Moffat (27 June 1944), p. 2.
32. "There is a tendency for 'crystal ball' organizations and 'think groups,' when they are established within the government bureaucracy, to become embroiled in 'putting out fires,' and to lose their intended purpose." Wesley W. Posvar, "Strategy Expertise and National Security" (Ph.D. diss., Harvard University, 1964), p. 59. See also Henry A. Kissinger, "The Policymaker and the Intellectual," in *The Necessity for Choice: Prospects of American Foreign Policy* (New York: Harper, 1960), pp. 340–58.

PWD was a separate division within the Air Staff, Plans, and was clearly labelled "Post War Division." If this division had been a subordinate branch of one of the other divisions within Plans (Combined and Joint Staff Division, Logistics Division, Strategy Division), its ability to remain aloof from the problems of fighting the war might have been lost. The fourth, and most important, factor was the underlying rationale for such a division. It was considered the autonomy division in that almost all AAF agencies which had contact with it treated it as the agency which would organize the case for autonomy. To burden it with the immediate problems of fighting the war would have hampered its efforts to create a fully coordinated, documented, and rational plan for Air Force autonomy in the postwar world.[33]

The focus of attention for the postwar planners as understood by Arnold, Kuter, and Moffat was planning for Air Force independence from the United States Army. Since Air Force autonomy was the primary concern for the planners, other factors such as doctrine, base requirements, and weapons systems forecasts were secondary considerations which could be modified in the interest of strengthening the AAF aim. The postwar planning for the organizational independence of the Air Force was thorough, detailed, and well-conceived, while that for international contingencies, though considerable, suffered from this concentration on the organizational aspects of the postwar military structure.

33. Kuter interview.

2

The Goal of Autonomy

Since the postwar goal of organizational independence of the Air Force was foremost in the minds of the AAF planners and leaders alike, the various plans written during the 1943–45 period can be fully understood only if this desire for autonomy is kept in mind.   What the postwar world situation might hold in the way of threats to American national security was, of course, of considerable concern to the postwar planners. What was of greater concern, however, was how the AAF could justify its case for autonomy in the immediate postwar period.   There were numerous plans written by the PWD, each based on a different set of specific assumptions, yet all were designed primarily to justify the case for an autonomous Air Force within the national defense structure of the United States.

The AAF leaders were unanimously for autonomy in the 1943–45 period for many reasons, each of which reinforced the others.   The primary reason was no longer what it had been in the 1930's, though the arguments differed only slightly from those of the earlier period.   In the 1930's the goal had been to claim one-third of the defense budget, while in the latter part of the war the aim was to capture all of it, or at least to become pre-eminent within the defense establishment.

The argument put forward in the plans, in the press, and before Congress was that autonomy was necessary since the air was a separate environment from the land or the sea, and that a cabinet-level equality with the Army and the Navy was thus also necessary.   In this justification for autonomy there was no evidence of any deviation from the arguments of the 1920's and 1930's.   It was when the Air Force leaders expanded upon this with a discussion of the strategic impact of technological developments in aeronautics that the pre-eminence of airpower in the accomplishment of national defense was hinted at by some and hammered at by others.

Certainly Colonel William Mitchell had claimed that airpower was the first line of defense and offense, but the Air Corps leaders of the 1920's and 1930's had been much more subtle in their arguments for autonomy. As World War II drew to a close, subtlety had largely disappeared and the obsolescence of navies and armies was pointed out by key AAF commanders such as Lieutenant General James Doolittle and General George Kenney.   They claimed that they wanted equality with the Army and Navy, but in making their case before Congress and the press their arguments were such that they could justify not equality but supremacy of the Air Force.

The arguments for airpower supremacy, which had been largely muted within the Air Corps since the Billy Mitchell trial of 1925, reappeared in greater strength. Although the explosion of the atomic bomb over Hiroshima was important, the official case for supremacy had already been made before the postwar planners knew of the new weapon. In their view the bomb did not make their case but only added weight to the argument for a carefully constructed program of national defense through strategic airpower.

The atomic bomb had no effect on AAF postwar planning prior to 6 August 1945 because no PWD officer knew of either the Manhattan Project or the atomic device.[1] General Kuter knew of atomic bomb development, as did a number of very senior Air Force officers, but he did not inform Colonel Moffat or any of the postwar planners for two reasons.[2] Information on the atomic device was restricted to those who held a specific clearance from President Roosevelt to information about the Manhattan Project; no one in the PWD held this clearance. Kuter also felt that it would be unwise to base postwar planning on the assumption that the United States would possess atomic weapons since there was no assurance during his tenure as Assistant Chief of Air Staff, Plans, that the Manhattan Project would produce a weapon of any military significance.[3] Norstad considered giving the postwar planners some information concerning the A-bomb but was sure that the President would not grant clearance to them.[4]

Although Major General Leslie R. Groves was given the authority to grant security clearances to persons working on the Manhattan Project, Roosevelt maintained control over the granting of clearances to persons not directly involved with the development of the atomic weapon.[5] In the words of General Groves: "For reasons of military security, we had always made a determined effort to withhold all information on the atomic bomb project from anyone, including members of the Executive Department, military personnel and members of Congress, except those who definitely needed it and who were authorized to receive it."[6]

Thus, the Hiroshima explosion was a complete surprise to all the postwar planners. As they looked at their plans in the light of this revolutionary development, they found that the A-bomb reinforced the emphasis on strategic bombardment that had been prominent in their planning since the autumn of 1943. The influence of the atomic bomb was important in that, prior to 6 August 1945, the planners had seen

1. For a discussion by the man in charge of the Manhattan Project which led to the development of the atomic bomb, see Leslie R. Groves, *Now It Can Be Told: The Story of the Manhattan Project* (New York: Harper, 1962).

2. The list of Army Air Force officers holding clearance to information concerning the development of atomic weapons was a short one. It included Arnold, Giles, Kuter, Eaker, and Spaatz, but did not include some AAF officers who held important positions in Headquarters during the war, such as Davison, Cabell, F. H. Smith, Jr., Dean, and Moffat.

3. Kuter interview.

4. Norstad interview.

5. Interviews with Norstad, Dean, and F. H. Smith, Jr.

6. Groves, *Now It Can Be Told*, p. 360.

American strategic bombardment as the guarantee of world peace, whereas it now ensured world peace in the eyes of most Americans. To the AAF leaders, the strategic bombardment mission for years had been both a means and an end. It was a means by which autonomy might be justified and obtained, but it was also considered by the AAF leaders to be the primary purpose of military aviation. The dual technological breakthrough of very-long-range bombers and atomic weapons made the strategic aviation enthusiasts of the past appear quite prophetic to the American public.

The serious questioning of the decisiveness and importance of strategic bombardment which was beginning to take place as the United States Strategic Bombing Survey reports were being completed never became a significant public issue. No matter how ill-conceived the Combined Bomber Offensive against Germany or the strategic offensive in the Pacific had been, it all became irrelevant to the American public, Congress, and the Air Force. Overnight, strategic bombardment had gone from thousand-plane missions with hundreds of escort fighters to a single bomber dropping a single bomb. Strategic bombardment had won its case, and the ignored lessons of World War II could remain ignored by the public, Congress, the Air Force, and all others except the inquiring scholar or the parochial Army or Navy man.

Why the AAF planners chose a combination of autonomy and unification rather than some other goal for the immediate postwar period warrants consideration.

Rear Admiral Forrest Sherman suggested that it might be wise for the AAF to remain in the Army since technological developments would soon allow the Air Force to exercise leadership within, and to dominate the policies of, the Army.[7] Why, indeed, should the Air Force be satisfied with one-third of the defense budget when it might have one-half by remaining in the Army?

The possibility of a fruitful alliance with the Army after the Air Force gained autonomy, to give the Air Force a two-to-one advantage over the Navy in any confrontation, was certainly a consideration, at least to Arnold, whose relationship with Marshall was one of close alliance, mutual respect, and admiration. Of greater importance, however, was the gyroscopic Air Corps policy of autonomy. Lieutenant General Dean, who spent much of the war as a member of Arnold's Advisory Council, felt that autonomy was the first priority for the postwar period for all AAF leaders.[8] To give up this dream just when attainment seemed so near could be contemplated by Admiral Sherman but was incomprehensible to Air Corps leaders.

---

7. "I personally am inclined to view that through a process of evolution if the present organization should continue, the air forces would dominate the Army." Testimony of Rear Admiral Forrest Sherman, U.S. Senate, Committee on Military Affairs, *Hearings on S.84 and S.1482, Unification of Armed Forces,* 79th Cong., 1st sess., 1945, p. 511.
8. Dean interview.

The coincidence of opinion within the Air Corps on the supreme importance of autonomy can be explained by years of frustrated efforts, the common bond of the joy of aviation, and the crusading attitude of these men. At last the tenuous theoretical arguments of Douhet and Mitchell had been justified in the eyes of the Air Corps leaders and the years of frustration were over. The great joy and overstatement in the period immediately following the successful explosion of the two atomic bombs was well recorded in the press and in the congressional hearings of 1945 and 1946. Airpower would defend this nation; airpower would guarantee the success of a new international security organization; airpower would punish aggression wherever it might manifest itself; airpower would save the world. Salvation had come; all America and the world needed to do was to maintain and support a strong United States Air Force—a simple, reliable formula. The airplane was not considered just another weapon; it was the ultimate weapon for universal peacekeeping.

Objectivity about this weapon was absent within Air Corps circles for many reasons. Perhaps the foremost reason was the psychological attachment of the airman to his machine. To him the airplane was not just a new and exciting weapon; it was what carried him miles behind enemy lines and brought him back; it was a personal possession which was given a personal, usually feminine, name, kissed upon return from a mission, and painted with a symbol for each enemy plane shot down or bombing mission completed.[9] The affinity of pilot for airplane has its parallel in history in the cavalry soldier and his horse. The airman, like the cavalryman of the past, was not known for his modesty, or his objectivity, when it came to the employment of his chosen steed.[10]

Secretary of the Navy James Forrestal asked Ferdinand Eberstadt, a close personal friend and former business associate, to undertake a study to determine the nation's best means for organizing itself for war. Eberstadt, a man with a reputation for independent thought, initiated the study in May 1945 and completed it in October 1945. He recommended a national defense establishment with three separate services, one of which was to be the Air Force, but there was a fear within the Navy's military and civilian leadership that autonomy for the Air Force would present dangers that might be avoided if the AAF remained within the War Department.[11] If the Navy supported the thesis that airpower was a

9. Douglas D. Bond, M.D., *The Love and Fear of Flying* (New York: International Universities Press, 1952), pp. 18–21.

10. Denis Healey, present Secretary of State for Defence, Great Britain, has described the nuclear missile as the phallic symbol of the 1960's. Lecture at Columbia University (24 March 1964). The cockpit of the airplane has also been described in Freudian terms; there is a theory among experts in flying safety in the USAF that the reason some pilots refuse to eject from crippled aircraft is a psychological confusion between the cockpit and the womb. *Flying Safety* (September 1958), p. 9. See also Anchara F. Zeller, "Psychological Factors in Escape" (United States Air Force Study, 1949).

11. Vincent Davis, *Postwar Defense Policy and the U.S. Navy, 1943–1946* (Chapel Hill: University of North Carolina Press, 1966), p. 360.

military responsibility separate and distinct from the responsibilities of the Army and Navy, then justification for the maintenance of a naval air arm would become difficult. If, however, the Navy could show that the Air Force should remain under the War Department, then justification for a naval air arm would not be as difficult. The Navy strategy was twofold. One tack was to emphasize that a separate Air Force would neglect certain essential missions such as close support of ground troops.[12] The other approach was to establish an attitude of indifference toward Air Force autonomy and refer to that issue as a War Department problem which that department could handle in any manner it saw fit.[13] By considering the Air Force problem a War Department concern, the Navy could continue to differentiate between two primary services rather than among three.

By the summer of 1945 the Navy was acutely aware of the danger the Air Force posed. The Navy benefited from the fact that the Air Force was not yet autonomous and that it was placing first priority on freedom from the Army and lesser priorities on incorporating anti-aircraft artillery, air liaison, and naval aviation into the autonomous Air Force.[14]

The crusading AAF leaders wanted the whole airpower mission, but were willing to compromise to secure it. The Army leadership felt that autonomy for the AAF was inevitable and saw in an autonomous AAF a potential ally in any interservice struggle with the Navy.[15] There is some indication that the Army was willing to agree to an autonomous Air Force to prevent the kind of Air Corps domination of the Army that Rear Admiral Forrest Sherman predicted if the Air Corps remained within the War Department. The Army leadership also believed that the case for Air Force autonomy had been proved as a result of both the tactical and the strategic lessons of the war. Most AAF leaders felt that the primary aim was freedom of the Air Corps from the Army and that engaging in an encounter with the Navy at the same time was not wise. Generals Kenney and Doolittle, however, deprecated the Navy, claiming the aircraft carrier obsolescent and asserting that all airpower should be under the control of a single service, the Air Force. The AAF planners did not set their sights as high as these two leaders, however, either

---

12. Testimony of Lieutenant General Ray S. Geiger, Commanding General, Fleet Marine Force, Pacific, 7 December 1945, U.S. Senate, *Hearings on S.84 and S.1482*, p. 559.

13. "If it should be decided by the Congress that there shall be three coordinated armed services, the matter is basically, and should be handled as, a question of dividing the War Department into two parts. To that extent, the problem is chiefly a concern of the War Department." Admiral Ernest J. King's 23 October 1945 testimony, *ibid.*, p.124. See also Nimitz testimony, *ibid.*, p. 391.

14. For the most thorough discussion of Navy postwar planning, see Davis, *Postwar Defense Policy*.

15. "The question will really be reversed and become whether or not the ground forces should have autonomy." Testimony of Sherman, 30 November 1945, U.S. Senate, *Hearings on S.84 and S.1482*, p. 511.

before or after the explosion of the atomic bomb. Although one plan called for all air training to be done by the autonomous Air Force, the Navy was not to be deprived of the naval air arm, only the basic flight training of that arm.

In their concentration on the role that they were to play, the AAF planners failed to view the national defense picture in its entirety. They drew up alternative plans based on various budget and force structures, but they did not seriously consider organizational alternatives such as remaining under the War Department, or autonomy plus incorporation of all airpower (Navy, Marine, and Army) into the new Air Force. The goal sought was the extraction of as much as possible from the War Department, and there was no deviation from this goal from 1943 through the end of 1945. The Navy aviation leaders chose to remain in the Navy in hopes of dominating that branch, while the Army aviation leaders chose a combination of autonomy and unification, a solution which would guarantee at least one-third of the defense budget and perhaps a great deal more.

The AAF approached the postwar planning problem with considerable ambivalence when it came to relationships with the other services. The Army was suspect because of its long reluctance to grant the Army Air Corps the autonomy it had demanded since World War I. At the same time, the Army leadership since 1939 had shown a distinct willingness to grant autonomy to the Air Force and to give it an enormous amount of funds and support in the years immediately preceding the war as well as during the war itself. Little oversights by Army staff officers in Washington were often considered by the Air Corps leaders to be indications that the Army was not sincere in its espousal of full autonomy for the Air Force in the postwar world.[16]

Kuter's attitude during the 1943–45 period was one of great trust and admiration for Marshall and Wedemeyer but continued distrust of the second-echelon Army generals whose attitudes toward Air Force autonomy were either unknown or suspect.[17] The evidence is strong that Arnold considered the battle with the Army basically won, and that the service which he feared would attempt to usurp part or all of the Air Force mission was the Navy.[18] The Air Force second-echelon

16. "It was noted that the basic outline, dated 15 April 1944, of the Post-War Military Establishment contained no statement or assumption relative to reorganization of the armed services into a single Department of War or the question of whether the Post-War Air Force should be independent and co-equal with the Ground and Naval forces. On the other hand, the 'Expanded Outline' (Incl. 1 to Incl. 3) is obviously based upon the present organization of the Army (including Air, Ground and Service components)." Memorandum for the Chief of Staff, U.S. Army; Subject: Expansion of Outline of the Post-War Military Establishment, from Lieutenant General Barney M. Giles, Chief of Air Staff (5 September 1944), p. 1. 145.86–57; 4334–139.

17. Kuter interview.

18. In a 30 April 1944 letter to Eaker, Arnold commented on the complete accord between the Army and Army Air Corps on the postwar military structure. 168.49; 3–4711–5.

leaders in the field also envisaged the Navy as the chief rival.[19]   However, the Army Air Force planners never wavered from their fundamental focus on freedom from Army control.

At the beginning of the postwar planning period, Army Field Manual 100–20 was published in revised form to recognize an equal relationship between land and air power.   This revision was viewed as a considerable victory for the Air Force, for unlike other actions taken by Marshall to grant it greater autonomy, this was a written change in a most important Army manual.   (Field Manual 100–20, entitled *Command and Employment of Air Power*, was dated 21 July 1943.)[20]

General Kuter was instrumental in making this change, having just returned from North Africa and being intent on incorporating into Army doctrine the practice, developed on the western North Africa front, of having the Army field commander and the tactical Air Force commander on an equal basis, rather than having the air commander subordinate to the army commander.   In a 22 May 1943 press conference, Kuter praised this system and indicated his desire to have the lessons learned applied to Army doctrine on air–ground cooperation.   "It is intended that the lesson learned and the successful methods developed in air–ground cooperation shall be translated into the broad American air effort as quickly as possible."[21]

The postwar planners under Kuter entered the planning process with this victory freshly won, together with numerous other gains.   The list is too long to include each decision considered by the Air Corps leaders to be victories for the Air Force, but the major ones follow: the 12 January 1939 Roosevelt request to Congress for $3 hundred million for 3000 additional airplanes for the Army;[22] the 16 May 1940

19. Reporting on a meeting on training held in July 1944 in San Francisco (which included representatives from all AAF combat areas and training groups), Captain G. W. Ebey of the Post War Division commented: "There seemed to be general agreement about the advisability of a separate Air Force but there likewise seemed to be a harmony of opinion concerning the advisability of keeping an eye on the Navy.   Colonel Garland, of the 8th Air Force, indicated that unless the AAF was very efficient in its activities and very careful in its planning, the Navy would move into such a position of strength that it could readily dominate air activity." (16 August 1944), p. 9.   145.86–32; 4334–101.

20. "I know that you will be interested in going over FM 100–20 dated 21 July 1943, the first three lines of which read: '1. Relationship of Forces. -LAND POWER AND AIR POWER ARE CO-EQUAL AND INTERDEPENDENT FORCES; NEITHER IS AN AUXILIARY OF THE OTHER.'"   Letter from Major General Giles, Chief of Air Staff, to Brigadier General Davidson, Commanding General, 10th Air Force, 9 September 1943.   Kuter indicated that as a result of the North African experience he was able, by June 1943, to get the War Department to change its doctrine to read: ". . . Air Forces and Ground Forces will work coordinately and coequally, neither subordinate to the other."   Letter from Kuter to Air Marshal Lin A. Coningham, 29 June 1943.   Kuter Papers, 1943 box.   See also Kuter Papers, vol. III, part II, p. 53.

21. Kuter Papers, vol. II, part II, p. 47.

22. *The Public Papers and Addresses of Franklin D. Roosevelt, 1939, War and Neutrality* (New York: Harper, 1949), p. 72.

Roosevelt message to Congress stating, "I should like to see this nation geared up to the ability to turn out at least 50,000 planes a year. Furthermore, I believe that this nation should plan at this time a program that would provide us with 50,000 military and naval planes;"[23] the March 1941 action taken by Stimson to place the air arm under a single commander, followed shortly by the revival of the office of the Assistant Secretary of War for Air under Robert A. Lovett;[24] the creation of the Army Air Forces on 20 June 1941;[25] the acceptance of AWPD/1 by the War Department General Staff and by Marshall as the Air Annex to the War Department Plan for the conduct of the war;[26] and the appointment of Arnold as a member of the Combined Chiefs of Staff (January 1942) and of the Joint Chiefs of Staff (February 1942).[27]

Despite these steps toward an independent, large Air Force, many of the organizational changes, procurement priorities, and field practices were not formalized, and throughout the 1943–45 postwar planning period there were numerous references to the temporary nature of the AAF gains. Much of what was accomplished by Roosevelt and Marshall to grant greater autonomy to the AAF was based on the war powers of the President, and there was continuing concern on the part of the AAF planners and leaders that six months after hostilities ceased the Air Force would revert to its 1939 position of subservience to the War Department. This concern, together with occasional slights by the War Department planners within the SPD, made the postwar planners continue to place autonomy, based on legislation, first in their order of priorities. Autonomy within a unified military service under a single Secretary of the Armed Forces and a single Commander of the Armed Forces or autonomy based on three coequal military services were the two alternatives considered by them. There is no evidence that they preferred unification, but the initial planning was based on the earlier War Department assumption that unification would take place in the immediate postwar period.

Intraservice (as opposed to interservice) rivalry and debate, which were present within the Army as a whole in the twenties and thirties and which served the useful purpose of questioning the doctrine of various service arms, were largely absent within the AAF. In the 1930's intraservice rivalry did bring into serious question the efficacy of coast artillery and horse-mounted cavalry and, in turn, inspired the Coast

23. *The Public Papers, 1940, War and Aid to Democracies*, p. 202.
24. Wesley Frank Craven and James Lea Cate, eds., *The Army Air Forces in World War II*, I, 115.
25. *Ibid.*
26. Lecture by H. S. Hansell, "Strategic Air Warfare," 1966 (exact date unknown). AWPD/1 was the plan authored by George, Walker, Kuter, and Hansell, four officers who had long experience at the ACTS in the 1930's; all four were firmly committed to the bombardment mission. This plan called for 100,000 planes, 2,100,000 men, and emphasis on the strategic bombardment mission.
27. Craven and Cate, *The Army Air Forces*, I, 254.

Artillery and the Cavalry to turn to weapons systems which they could more easily justify—the anti-aircraft artillery gun and the tank.[28]

Discussion of this rivalry leads to the obvious question of whether constructive intraservice debate can exist within an arm that is not an independent service. In the twenties and thirties, the infantry questioned the efficacy of the horse, the air corps questioned the value of the coast artillery gun, and neither cavalry nor coast artillery modified their weapons systems until they felt threatened by outside forces within the Army. The difficulty involved in evoking intraservice debate within an arm that is not a separate service (which may be called intra-intra-service rivalry) is the strong allegiance to an arm. In a large military service, the primary identification is usually with an arm of that service and not with the service itself (a man is a submariner, a naval aviator, a cavalryman, an infantryman) because of the tendency to identify with some smaller and more personal group. Once this identification is made, then the possibility of criticizing the service in general or another arm of the same service is open. By the same token, criticism of the arm that the individual has identified himself with becomes more difficult, and the benefits of interservice and intraservice debate do not normally extend to the arm itself. As the Army Air Corps slowly developed separateness, it did not at the same time develop the intraservice debate that was to blossom in the period following formal autonomy. In this period of unformalized autonomy, the only voices questioning the dominant AAF doctrine came from outside the Air Force.

Colonel S. F. Giffin, who prior to the war had been an instructor in the Department of Economics, Government and History at the United States Military Academy, in a lengthy memorandum entitled "Future Trends in Air Fighting" attempted to point out the postwar requirement for tactical aviation.[29] Colonel Giffin thought it unhealthy that there was no voice in the Air Force for fighter aviation.[30] He attempted to fill that gap by arguing that the great unlearned lessons of World War II were the offensive and great range capability of the fighter aircraft, its ability to destroy enemy aviation in the air and on the ground, and its effectiveness as an offensive weapon against tactical and strategic targets. He argued that the postwar Air Force should have at least twice as many fighter groups as bomber groups since fighters were needed for escort (on a one-to-one basis with bombers), for air defense, for close support of ground troops, and for strategic sweeps. In Giffin's words: "I believe it to be an unhealthy thing that within the Air Force itself there is presently

---

28. A study of technological obsolescence within the United States military, though beyond the scope of this book, might prove extremely insightful. A comparative study of the horse cavalry, the coast artillery, and the strategic bomber in order to ascertain the techniques used to justify the retention of obsolescent weapons systems might be a useful approach.

29. Memorandum for General Donald Wilson (25 November 1944). 145.86–100; 2–2210–15-25.

30. *Ibid.*, p. 2.

so little difference of opinion as regards the future course of air warfare and the line which we must take in creating the future Air Force. We are committed to the big bomber and the bomber offensive as surely for the future as we have been throughout this war, and with scarcely a dissenting voice." [31]

Kuter rejected Giffin's analysis in the following manner:

> I feel that Col. Giffin's points are well taken with reference to the next year or two but do not go along with him on the longer range consideration. I feel sure that the fighter will go into the strategic air offensive in Europe and in Japan, but that a weapon much more similar to our present VHB than to our present fighter is the longer time backbone of air power. [32]

Giffin's rather prophetic ideas were dismissed easily for two reasons. First, Kuter realized that strategic bombardment doctrine was so firmly established within the leadership of the AAF that Giffin's comments could be rejected without concern that a high-ranking Air Corps officer might use his arguments to modify the planned postwar Air Force structure. Also, Giffin was a Coast Artillery officer who had only recently transferred to the Air Corps—he was not a pilot and had not attended the Air Corps Tactical School at Maxwell AFB; he could be and *was* ignored since he lacked the qualifications to make his voice heard as an aviation expert. Had he solicited the support of a high-ranking Air Corps officer who was not firmly committed to the doctrine of strategic bombardment, his ideas might have received more than the summary dismissal they got. In Washington, during the entire war, there were no high-ranking Air Corps officers who questioned strategic bombardment and it would have been difficult for Giffin or any other critic of AAF doctrine to use a combat commander with a commitment to tactical aviation, such as Generals Kenney, Quesada, Griswold, or Saville, since their influence on postwar planning was minimal. [33]

Throughout the entire planning period, the only written espousal of fighter as opposed to bomber aviation that went beyond the role of fighters as long-range escorts for bombers was the Giffin memorandum. Giffin realized that he was opposing established doctrine—his opening sentence read: "The purpose of this memorandum is to preach heresy." [34] Heresy is exactly what he was preaching, for the long period of frustration within the Army Air Corps had converted doctrine into dogma. To question the big bomber was to question not doctrine but sacred dogma. Giffin was not burned at the stake; he was completely ignored as an

---

31. *Ibid.*
32. Note attached to the Giffin memorandum (5 December 1944).
33. General Kenney was unsuccessful in his effort to obtain B-29's for his command. Smith interview. There was no case in the entire war in which Arnold permitted large numbers of strategic bombers to come under the command of any individual who was not committed to the strategic utilization of bombardment aircraft.
34. The Giffin memorandum, p. 1. There is no evidence in the AAF files that Giffin made these same points to interested Army staff officers.

unqualified outsider. There is some irony in the fact that Giffin's memorandum was addressed to General Wilson, one of the earliest protagonists for precision strategic bombardment. Wilson was the head of the Air Corps Board, a board of officers located at Orlando, Florida, which studied AAF training, operational, doctrinal, and technological problems and made recommendations for improvements in these areas to Arnold and the Air Staff. By getting deeply involved in technological matters (such as bomb-sight deficiencies and bomber turret locations), the Air Corps Board was not an effective advisory group to Arnold and the Air Staff on matters of broad wartime and postwar policy.

The AAF, being a separate service without formal autonomy, presented its leaders with a dilemma: Should intraservice rivalry among various Army Air Corps factions (bombardment, pursuit, attack) be permitted and encouraged to avoid neglecting any airpower technological breakthrough, or should intraservice rivalry be suppressed in the interest of presenting a united front for autonomy? The habits and the rationale of the 1930's continued throughout the war; that is, the fighter enthusiast was isolated by being placed firmly under the control of a bombardment leader, by being sent to an insignificant (or less significant) theater of operations, or by tacit bribery through the encouragement of long-range fighter development. The fighter enthusiasts' dilemma was the conflicting desire for autonomy and fighter development. At times, the fighter leaders would place autonomy ahead of fighter development; at other times, they would use alliances with ground commanders to push fighter development to the possible detriment of autonomy. Bombardment and autonomy were natural partners, but fighters were antithetical to both except when fighters were used to support the strategic mission.

In the 1943–45 period, the fighter leaders were, in general, willing to accept less than they desired in order to win autonomy. Intraservice rivalry from 1943 to 1945 was practically nonexistent, and the voices that had been raised for fighter aviation were silenced by the bombardment leaders' acceptance of the requirement for a long-range fighter escort of bombardment aircraft. One great lesson the experience seems to illustrate is the need for intraservice competition to encourage doctrine to develop which is firmly based on the realities of technology. The doctrine that was the basis for postwar planning from 1943 through 1945 was that of the middle thirties modified to incorporate the long-range escort fighter.

Just as Air Corps leaders in the late 1930's were unwilling to observe technological developments in pursuit aircraft and just as Air Corps leaders in the early 1940's refused to recognize that development in German defensive tactics and technology might proceed at a faster pace than offensive tactics and technology, the postwar planners seemed unable even to contemplate the possibility that air defense might ever gain an ascendancy over air offense. Considering that the AAF planners worked without knowledge of the atomic weapon, they developed a force structure that ignored every air lesson of World War II save the need for long-range escort.

If intraservice competition had existed in the 1930's, it probably would have continued into the 1940's, and a voice like that of Colonel Giffin might have been heard. Such competition was essentially non-existent in the interwar period largely because the Army Air Corps leadership did not consider the Army Air Corps a separate service.[35] Those who might have defended pursuit aviation and pointed out the vulnerabilities of bombardment aircraft as well as the deficiencies of daylight precision bombing theory were silent for two reasons. They had no platform and they did not wish to sabotage the greater goal—autonomy.[36]

35. Huntington calls the Army Air Corps of the 1930's a "semi-service." Samuel P. Huntington, "Inter-Service Competition and the Political Roles of the Armed Services," *Problems of National Strategy: A Book of Readings*, ed. Henry A. Kissinger (New York: Praeger, 1965), p. 452.

36. Huntington points out that intraservice competition is subordinate to inter-service competition. Samuel P. Huntington, *The Common Defense: Strategic Programs in National Politics* (New York: Columbia University Press, 1961), p. 407. Although identification with an arm or branch of the service creates the fundamental environment for intraservice rivalry, this case study substantiates Huntington's thesis that, "For no service was intraservice competition ever equal in importance to competition among the services." *Ibid.*

3

The Role of Doctrine

Air Corps doctrine in the 1930's and during the war was basically the same, and it was based primarily on the concept of the decisiveness of strategic bombardment in war. Although there may be some question as to whether, in the thirties, this doctrine was used to justify the Army Air Corps case for autonomy or whether autonomy was a means the Army Air Corps leadership tried to use to insure that American military airpower would be heavily weighted in favor of the strategic bombing mission, the evidence indicates that in the 1943–45 period the former was the case. Since their goal could best be supported if the efficacy and decisiveness of strategic airpower in war could be fully demonstrated, any arguments concerning the necessity for tactical aviation in support of ground warfare would undermine their case. Therefore, the doctrine and the decisiveness of strategic bombardment in future warfare were inextricably tied to the AAF case for autonomy. If strategic bombardment could not be decisive in warfare, and if victory could be obtained only by having an army actually meet and defeat the enemy on the battlefield, then it would be difficult to refute the case for maintaining within the United States Army the Army Air Corps (with its missions of close support of ground troops and interdiction of lines of communication) in order to support the majority of this nation's forces.

If the AAF postwar planners had had as their primary goal the independence of the strategic element of military airpower, the value of tactical aviation could still have been acknowledged by them without undermining their position that strategic bombardment was a mission distinct from the mission of the ground army. However, since they wanted to place all land-based military airpower in the autonomous postwar Air Force, acknowledgment of any tactical aviation doctrine would have weakened their case. The relationship between doctrine and force structure within the prewar Air Corps had caused its leadership to neglect some important technological breakthroughs in pursuit aviation. The narrow doctrinal focus which the postwar planners felt obliged to maintain to achieve autonomy was no more than a continuation of inflexible prewar thinking.

A long-time student of airpower, Professor William R. Emerson, has observed: "Making all due allowances for the difficulties and the genuine accomplishments of our strategists, it should, nevertheless, be perfectly clear that every salient belief of prewar American air doctrine was either overthrown or drastically modified by the experience of war." [1]

1. William R. Emerson, "Operation Pointblank: A Tale of Bombers and Fighters" (United States Air Force Academy, The Harmon Memorial Lectures in Military History, no. 4, 1962), p. 40.

What Emerson fails to mention is that the lessons learned about the limitations of strategic aviation were not applied to the formulation of the postwar Air Force. Instead of making the common mistake of planning to fight the next war with weapons and techniques that had been effective in the last, the Air Corps planners were laying plans to conduct the next war using weapons and techniques that had been proven largely ineffective in the present war. The reason is quite obvious: the planners were not making detailed plans for fighting the next war but rather were planning for a force that could provide the justification for autonomy. The doctrinal dedication to strategic bombardment at the expense of close air support and interdiction led to difficulties, among them lack of adequate support of ground forces during the Korean conflict, de-emphasis of tactical training, and lack of development of tactical weapons systems and tactical munitions (much of the development in these areas was done by the Navy in the two decades following World War II).

To understand the assumptions made, and the doctrine upon which the postwar force structure was based, it is useful to trace the doctrinal development of the United States military strategic bombardment theory. This theory, developed in the twenties and thirties and fully incorporated in the major Army Air Corps prewar plan, AWPD/1, can best be described as modified Douhet. Recent evidence confirms the direct Douhetan input into the Tactical School as early as 1923, but the doctrine that was fully developed by 1940 was Douhetan, modified in a number of significant areas.[2] Douhet's tenets that the air weapon was strongly offensive, that technology favored the defensive on land and sea, and that airpower alone could bring victory were fully accepted Army Air Corps doctrine.[3] Not all of Douhet was incorporated; his gross exaggeration of bomb damage was rejected by the Tactical School by 1938,[4] and by 1939 the school no longer recognized as valid his belief that enemy morale was an effective target. The abandonment of the undermining of civilian morale as a useful aim of bombardment was a result of a 1939 lecture presented at the Tactical School, which made the point that Chinese morale and the will to resist increased as a result of Japanese bombardment.[5]

2. See above, p. 8.
3. AWPD/1 gives the best indication of Army Air Corps doctrine just prior to the commencement of World War II (it must be noted that Army Air Corps doctrine was not Army doctrine). "AWPD-1 was almost straight Pre-War Tactical School doctrine." H. S. Hansell lecture to Air War College, "The Development of the U.S. Concept of Bombardment Operations" (12 November 1953), p. 502.
4. Kuter, in a lecture entitled "American Air Power—School Theories vs. World War Facts," which he wrote and delivered in 1938 to the students of the Air Corps Tactical School, acknowledged some limitations in strategic aviation.
"The Mystery Bomber may have come 10,000 miles through the stratosphere at the velocity of sound . . . but the power it can apply to the bridge is absolutely unchanged and many defensive measures must now be overcome." [Kuter's ellipsis.] "Let us start with the honest admission that the bomb of today is no more powerful than similar bombs of the World War." Kuter Papers, vol. II, part II, p. 13.
5. Joe Gray Taylor, "They Taught Tactics," *Aerospace Historian*, XIII (Summer 1966), 68.

In addition to these differences, Douhet's vagueness on target selection had been replaced by an explicit doctrine of bombardment based on the thesis that precision bombardment would allow specific targets to be attacked and that a nation's economy could be totally incapacitated by the careful selection and elimination of a few essential industries. Captain (later Major General) Donald Wilson is usually credited with establishing this theory of economic vulnerability which by the late 1930's was fully accepted as Air Corps doctrine.[6] The theory had a certain validity but was expressed in such a generalized form that the economic principle of "substitution" was ignored. In a 1933 lecture at the Tactical School, Wilson stated that transportation and electric generator manufacturing plants were considered key components of a nation's economy, and that "it would seem obvious that any air force worthy of the name should be able to destroy faster than replacement could be effected."[7] By considering a nation's economy a "structure" rather than a set of activities which could be undertaken in a wide variety of ways, the instructors at the Tactical School demonstrated an unsophisticated grasp of macroeconomics. "The fault was one of economics, not airmanship."[8] I. B. Holley points out that without "a doctrine regarding the use of weapons..."[9] there has been a great reluctance on the part of both military and civilian leaders in many states to develop and use new and superior weapons. "New weapons when not accompanied by correspondingly new adjustments in doctrine are just so many external accretions in the body of an army."[10]

The Army Air Corps leadership firmly believed that superior arms favor victory; they recognized the relationship between doctrine and weaponry; and they understood the need for effective techniques for recognizing and evaluating potential weapons.[11] Unfortunately, their focus both before and during World War II was narrow, so that only ideas and weaponry which favored the offensive role of aviation were given thorough consideration. The doctrine developed in the Air Corps Tactical School from 1926 through 1940 was not airpower doctrine in its

6. Wilson takes credit for initiating this theory into the Air Corps Tactical School. Donald Wilson, "Origin of a Theory for Air Strategy" (typewritten study, 1962), p. 3. See also Robert T. Finney, *History of the Air Corps Tactical School, 1920–1940* (Maxwell Air Force Base, Montgomery, Ala.: USAF Historical Study No. 100, 1955), pp. 31–32.

7. Wilson, "Origin of a Theory," p. 2.

8. Mancur Olson, Jr., "The Economics of Strategic Bombing in World War II," *Airpower Historian*, IX (April 1962), 123.

9. Irving B. Holley, *Ideas and Weapons* (New Haven: Yale University Press, 1953), p. 10.

10. *Ibid.*, p. 14.

11. Holley indicates that throughout history there have been three specific shortcomings in the procedure for developing new weapons, "... a failure to adapt, actively and positively, the thesis that superior arms favor victory; a failure to recognize the importance of establishing a doctrine regarding the use of weapons; and a failure to devise effective techniques for recognizing and evaluating potential weapons in the advances of science and technology." *Ibid.*, p. 10.

broadest sense of the word "airpower." It was strategic, daylight, precision bombardment, a very important part, but only a part, of military aviation. The emphasis on bombardment made the Tactical School instructors acutely aware of technological advances in this area, such as the development of bomb-sight equipment which permitted bombing accuracy from altitudes over 25,000 feet, and improvements in engine and airframe construction which permitted considerable advancement in bomber range, speed, and altitude capabilities during the 1930's. The familiarity with the technological developments in bombardment aviation within the Tactical School in the twenties and thirties, among the AAF leadership prior to and during the war, and among the AAF planners during the war was exceptional (though the PWD was unaware of atomic developments prior to 6 August 1945).[12]   Yet the narrow focus of prewar Air Corps planners and leaders made these officers unaware of aircraft developments outside the strategic mission.   Although the retarded development within the Army Air Corps throughout the thirties of radar, the air-cooled engine, and the long-range fighter is beyond the scope of this book, it should be pointed out that the narrow doctrinal focus, which inhibited these developments, continued throughout the entire war within the Air Force operational and postwar planning offices.[13]

Once a military doctrine is established it is difficult to change, especially if technological advancements in weaponry seriously bring into question a doctrine upon which a specific military service is based. Like policy, doctrine has a gyroscopic effect.   And if service doctrine is questioned by members of that service, there is a tendency for the leadership to brand the critics heretics, especially if the doctrine is the basis upon which the primary goals of a service are constructed.   In addition, the formulation and articulation of the doctrine is ordinarily designed to justify fully the service's attempt to obtain or maintain exclusive control over certain missions.   Criticism usually results in an undermining of the case the service has so carefully made for certain roles and missions in national defense.   Dissent is therefore discouraged, and breakthroughs in technology which might bring established doctrine into question are often ignored.

It is unfair to say that Arnold and other Air Force leaders completely ignored the vulnerability of long-range bombardment aircraft to defensive fighter attack, or that they were totally unaware of the lessons of the Battle of Britain regarding the technological advances in pursuit aviation. What was ignored or overlooked was the possibility of building a long-range escort fighter which would be essentially a pursuit aircraft and not a heavily armed bomber.[14]   While the Air Force leaders understood the value of the four-engine bomber and its advantages in range, capacity,

12. Interviews with Kuter, Norstad, Smith, and Cabell.
13. For some interesting insights into the relationship between doctrine and weaponry, see Bernard Boylan, *Development of the Long-Range Escort Fighter* (Maxwell Air Force Base, Montgomery, Ala.: USAF Historical Study No. 136, 1955).
14. *Ibid.*, pp. 33–35.

reliability, and defensive firepower over the two-engine bomber (in the words of two eminent students of the AAF, "The Army airman thereafter was, above all else, an advocate of the big bomber, and around the potentialities of that type of plane he built his most cherished hopes." [15]), these same leaders almost totally ignored the advances being made in pursuit aviation—advances that were even greater than those made in bombardment aviation. [16] Among these were the increased speed, altitude, and range capabilities of projected fighter aircraft. The neglect by the Air Corps leaders of technological developments in pursuit aviation, from 1935 to 1943, provides an interesting case study of the relationship between doctrine and force structure. The postwar planners made a similar error for the same basic reason. They neglected tactical aviation in their postwar force structure because of their doctrinal focus upon strategic aviation. The story of the retarded development of the long-range fighter escort mission will be briefly traced to illustrate the continuity of the Air Corps planners' focus from 1935 through 1945, as well as to illustrate how doctrine affects force structure and can undermine objectivity.

Air Corps leaders had reached a doctrinal decision by 1935 as to the efficacy of unescorted long-range strategic bombardment and were unwilling either to question that decision or even to observe technological advances that might cause them to modify this doctrine until 1943 when the whole concept of strategic bombardment was endangered by the horrendous losses over Germany. It is paradoxical that their total acceptance of the doctrine prevented them from observing the technological advances that would have been the salvation of the very concept they were proclaiming. From 1931 until 1938 the bombardment advocates denied pursuit aviation any role other than the harassment of enemy bombers. The more radical even advocated the discontinuation of all pursuit procurement. The official Air Force history on the development of air doctrine during this period states that, "Coupled with the apparent authority in performance of the new bombers over existing pursuit, acceptance of Douhet led the bombardment enthusiasts to an extreme position. Some instructors at the ACTS believed that pursuit could be abolished altogether, and OCAC [Office of Chief of Air Corps] adopted the slogan, 'Fighters are obsolete.'" [17] By 1938, however, the bombardment men were willing to admit that, through proper early warning, pursuit aircraft could not only harass but, if properly massed, might even disrupt the bombardment formation.

15. Wesley F. Craven and James L. Cate, eds., *The Army Air Forces in World War II* (Chicago: University of Chicago Press, 1948), I, 67.

16. In the fall of 1941 General Kuter wrote a memorandum entitled "Reference Data on Heavy Bombers," in which he pointed out seventeen reasons why "big bombardment airplanes are better than little bombardment air planes...." Some of Kuter's reasons are of interest: for example, "6. The big bomber can defend itself...; 8. The big bomber can work alone...." 168.80–1; 5–2405–2.

17. Thomas H. Greer, *The Development of Air Doctrine in the Army Air Arm, 1917–1941* (Maxwell Air Force Base, Montgomery, Ala.: USAF Historical Study No. 89, 1955), p. 45.

"Major Harold L. George, on 26 December 1937, advised Maj. Gen. Delos C. Emmons, Commander of GHQ Air Force, that there was no question in his mind that American bombardment units were defenseless against American pursuit groups." [18]

An interesting facet of this realization of the increasing danger presented by defensive fighters is the solutions that were sought. Instead of checking with the aircraft companies or with the Air Corps development center at Dayton, Ohio, the Army Air Corps leaders became their own amateur aeronautical engineers and arrived at the idea of a heavily armored bomber aircraft with enormous defensive firepower. (In fact, Douhet's idea of a combat plane was quite similar to the Air Corps idea of a heavily armored plane of bomber size designed to provide the defensive firepower needed to protect bomber formations.) [19] The Air Corps leaders advocated the use of very large masses of bombers which would force the enemy to split his defensive efforts and face as many as a thousand bombers in formation with coordinated defensive firepower. They also advocated better and more turrets, high-caliber machine guns, and other changes to the craft.

The idea of increasing the range of fighter aircraft to the point that it would approach that of the bomber was quickly rejected as impractical, without a systematic inquiry into the possibility. The Air Corps leaders were certainly technologically oriented (Arnold himself was the leader in his appreciation of the technological impact upon aviation), but their orientation was narrow in scope in that the questions asked were not how could the strategic mission be improved but what improvements could be made in the strategic aircraft. In this case, Arnold's grasp of technology, in conjunction with his doctrinal preconceptions, prevented him in 1939 from asking some key questions. Once aware of the improvements in defensive fighter capability, he should have asked two questions: Is the doctrine of strategic bombardment valid in light of the difficulties involved in delivering bombs against well-defended targets? In what way can the strategic bombardment mission be improved in order to insure its efficacy despite the defensive improvements previously observed?

This doctrinal commitment to strategic bombardment made the first question a difficult one for Arnold to ask, but the second question should have been much easier to examine in light of his admitted realization of the dangers bombers might expect to face. Yet there is no evidence, in the form of any systematic analysis of the various possibilities, that the second question was ever asked by Arnold or his immediate staff.

18. Boylan, *Long-Range Escort Fighter*, p. 33.

19. Giulio Douhet, *The Command of the Air*, trans. Sheila Fischer (Rome: Rivista Aeronautica, 1958), p. 97. For a discussion of the inadequacies of bombers modified to provide increased firepower as a means of protecting bomber formations, see Stephen P. Birdsall, "The Destroyer Escorts," *Airpower Historian*, XII (July 1965), 92–94. Also see Boylan, *Long-Range Escort Fighter*, pp. 136–46.

The British did ask the question and ordered the P-51 as a long-range escort fighter even though all evidence in the late thirties indicated that bomber losses at night would not approach daytime losses. The Army Air Corps leaders, facing the greater danger that daylight precision bombing would entail, did not seriously examine long-range fighter escort. What is evident here is British pragmatism versus American dogmatism, for the American Air Corps leaders in their fight for autonomy and for a strategic mission had found it advantageous to play down the role of pursuit, attack, liaison, and reconnaissance aviation. A recent study of the Tactical School concludes, "Attachment to this commitment [strategic bombardment] was, however, so inflexible that it inhibited the development of tactics for escort, for air defense, for support of ground forces and for reconnaissance and transport aviation. Thus the school's greatest achievement as a laboratory for Air Corps thought prevented the full accomplishment of the purpose designated by the name, the Air Corps Tactical School." [20] Even to ask whether fighter range could be increased to the point at which escort would be feasible was to indicate some questioning of the earlier statements about the need to abolish the pursuit mission. Overstatements made to sell bombardment in the 1935–38 period committed Air Corps leaders to a fixed view on how to execute the strategic mission.

The lack of a voice for pursuit aviation in the higher echelons of the Air Corps made the questioning of doctrine unlikely. Interestingly, every Air Corps leader had been a pursuit pilot, yet by the late 1930's the commitment to bombardment was almost complete. This is curious only in that these same men ignored the advances in the pursuit mission made in the late 1930's. Since there was no real bombardment mission in the Air Corps until the late 1920's, due to the lack of an aircraft that had the range, speed, and bomb-carrying capability to be called a bomber, the pursuit mission was the only mission the American Air Service had prior to the advent of the B-9 and B-10 bombers. [21]

The outspoken exponent of pursuit aviation during the crucial years of the 1930's, when the Army Air Corps was searching for a doctrine, was Claire Chennault. Holding a number of responsible positions at the Air Corps Tactical School, he provided both written and verbal opposition to prevalent ideas that pursuit aviation was obsolete. When Chennault retired as a Captain in 1937, the Army Air Corps lost its only articulate, albeit polemical, voice for fighter aviation. His career was a signal to the pursuit enthusiasts that advances in the Air Corps were not likely to be most rapid in those channels, and ambitious officers were quick to select the bombardment side of military flying.

There was enough outside emphasis from the ground Army officers

20. Taylor, "They Taught Tactics," p. 72. Taylor might have added liaison aviation also. I. B. Holley points out the neglect by the Army Air Corps of liaison aviation from 1920 to 1940 in *Evolution of the Liaison-Type Airplane: 1917–1944* (Washington: AAF Historical Study No. 44, 1946).

21. Greer, *Air Doctrine*, p. 45.

that the attack mission was never completely overlooked, but the pursuit mission had no real interest group to support it from 1931 to 1935 when bomber technology advanced more rapidly than did pursuit technology. Attack aviation had infantry support, and bombardment aviation had the support of all Air Corps men interested in autonomy. Pursuit aviation had a kind of negative support, since to support it doctrinally was to point out the vulnerabilities of bombardment aviation. If pursuit aviation enthusiasts could have supported their case by pointing out its value without explicitly or implicitly infringing on the sacred doctrine of bombardment aviation, perhaps their voice would have survived the technologically lean years.

To point out the vulnerabilities of strategic bombardment was to jeopardize the Air Corps case for autonomy, for if strategic bombardment was proved ineffective as the element of warfare which alone might prove to be decisive in battle, then its case would be seriously undermined. If flights of bombardment aircraft could be turned back, or if the defensive fighters could inflict unacceptable losses upon the bombing formation, then the whole concept of strategic bombardment would be proved erroneous, and the Air Corps would then be expected to accomplish only close support, air superiority, and interdiction, none of which (nor all in combination) could justify complete autonomy. In the history of military aviation (from 1907 until the present, except for the brief period from 1931 to 1935), pursuit aircraft have held an advantage over bombers in combat, where the latter have sustained heavier losses. Although the reasons for fighter superiority vary, the combination of higher altitude and speed capability, in addition to greater maneuverability, have usually given the advantage.

The quest for autonomy led to the advocacy of strategic bombardment, which led, in turn, to the deprecation of not only defensive pursuit aircraft but all pursuit aircraft. Bombardment and autonomy were so inextricably bound together that the questioning of bombardment by an Air Corps officer was not only impolitic but unwise. Chennault's memoirs, though definitely lacking objectivity, give some idea of the problems pursuit enthusiasts encountered in the 1930's.[22]

In the 1943–45 period, the postwar planners did not consider that the case for autonomy had been won. Although the wartime arrangements gave credence to the strong probability of obtaining autonomy in the immediate postwar world, the AAF planners were unwilling to assume that it was a certainty. First of all, the prewar laws which placed the Air Corps in a subordinate position to the Army were suspended for the duration of the war plus six months, and unless Congress acted quickly at the termination of hostilities, it appeared to the planners that the Air Corps might revert to its pre-World War II status. Second, there was a suspicion on the part of many of the leaders that the Army and the War Department were neither committed to nor enthusiastic

22. *Way of a Fighter: The Memoirs of Claire Lee Chennault*, ed. Robert Hartz (New York: G. P. Putnam's, 1949), pp. 3–31. See also Greer, *Air Doctrine*, pp. 58–65.

about a separate Air Force. The commitment to bombardment was therefore just as strong in the 1943–45 period as it had been previously, and the only evident variation was the commitment to long-range escort. The airpower lesson of the war up until 6 August 1945 was the efficacy of tactical aviation in its threefold mission of air superiority, interdiction, and close support of ground troops. Yet postwar planning was aimed at the strategic bombardment mission, with fighters provided primarily in the escort mission.[23] Walter Millis, an eminent student of the U.S. military, said:

> The one great, determining factor which shaped the course of the Second War was not, as is so often said and so generally believed, independent air power. It was the mechanization of the ground battlefield with automatic transport, with the "tactical" airplane and above all with the tank. Air power in its independent form was, in sober fact, relatively ineffective. It was the teaming of the internal combustion engine in the air and on the surface, in order to take the traditional objectives of surface warfare which, together with the remarkable development of electronic communications, really determined the history of the Second World War.[24]

Since the aim of the postwar planners was to plan for and justify an autonomous Air Force, and since this was the reason that Arnold "tolerated" the planners, it is understandable that they based their plans on theories of war causation, potential enemies, and base requirements which would best justify autonomy. (General Kuter believes that Arnold's attitude toward the planners was one of toleration rather than enthusiastic support.)[25] This is not to imply that the Air Force planners were cynics who were searching for ways to justify their existence. These men believed that airpower was the most effective way to maintain national security, but they came to this belief not by a scholarly weighing of a number of alternatives.

Although there is no evidence that the postwar planners relied on the strategic and political concepts of Alfred Thayer Mahan, the conceptual similarities between some of his ideas and their assumptions invite a hypothesis: a selective use of Mahan, adapted to justify not naval power but airpower, was the basis for many of the planners' assumptions concerning the economic causes of conflict and the causes of actual war.

With the substitution of the word "airpower" for the word "seapower," much of Mahan's writing becomes quite similar to AAF doctrine. Mahan used skillfully a theoretical construct to justify the building of a

23. "Our most persuasive and articulate people are almost without exception bomber minded." "I think it is self-evident that heavy bomber thinking continues to dominate the Air Force." "If the experience of the European air war means anything, we have not provided sufficient fighters in the post war air force." The Giffin memorandum.

24. Walter Millis, *Arms and Men: A Study in American Military History* (New York: G. P. Putnam's, 1956), p. 283.

25. Kuter interview.

large navy and to prove that navies would be decisive in warfare. The AAF planners wished to accomplish what Mahan had succeeded in doing for the Navy; they wanted to prove not only that the Air Force should be a separate, autonomous force but that it was America's first line of defense and *the* decisive element of the American military. Mahan, though a reluctant imperialist, was nevertheless an imperialist when it came to the acquiring of overseas bases.[26] The Air Force planners likewise were imperialists when it came to acquiring overseas air bases. The commercial aspects of naval and air bases were often emphasized, but military importance was always the primary consideration in their selection. Mahan's interpretation of history, in which he linked seapower with national greatness, and imperialism with seapower, affected the thinking of the wartime AAF planners, who wanted to secure bases in the Western Pacific, Alaska, Newfoundland, Iceland, Western Africa, and the Western Hemisphere. Like Mahan, the postwar planners were not unwilling to use coercion to acquire permanent bases.

Mahan's "principles" of naval strategy, which were largely based on Jomini's principles of war,[27] but modified to fit the peculiar problems of seapower, included the principle of concentration of force, a principle which the Air Force planners incorporated in all but one of their postwar plans.[28] These plans included a large reservoir of strategic aviation located within the United States. Mahan criticized the French for using their fleet as a defensive force and praised the British for using theirs to seek out the enemy or to trap his fleet in port where it could not protect its commercial vessels or control the sea. Mahan was contemptuous of the *guerre de course* and considered cruiser and commerce raiding operations the province of land warfare and hence a grave error in naval strategy.[29] Again a parallel is evident since the AAF leaders and planners were reluctant to divert airpower to the close support of troops or to the defensive role of interception.

When Mahan described the dominant characteristic required of a war fleet as not speed but "the power of offensive action,"[30] his approach was not dissimilar to the arguments in favor of the long-range super-fortress in great formations warding off the ineffective defensive forces with concentrated firepower and heavy armament. Douhet's combat plane and Kuter's battleplane were both somewhat similar to Mahan's heavy ships-of-the-line (the battleship or the capital ship). The similarity between Mahan's political defense of the nation through offensive use of the fleet and the proposed AAF defense through strategic bombardment is also evident.

26. Margaret Tuttle Sprout, "Mahan: Evangelist of Sea Power," in *Makers of Modern Strategy: Military Thought from Machiavelli to Hitler*, ed. Edward Mead Earle (Princeton: Princeton University Press, 1952), p. 429.
27. *Ibid.*, p. 431.
28. The exception was the Initial Post War Air Force Plan (105 groups).
29. Sprout, "Mahan," p. 433.
30. *Ibid.*

Mahan was unwilling to consider that the submarine or the airplane might be effective defense against the battle fleet; and AAF postwar planners were unwilling to see air defense, either aircraft, guided missile, or anti-aircraft as an effective defense against the escorted bomber formation. Mahan had shown how, in naval warfare, the best defense against attack was a concentrated offensive naval fleet. The airpower enthusiasts were quick to utilize this most logical argument to make a case for a preponderant offensive air-force-in-being as the first line of defense.

Even the tendency of Mahan to ignore technology was evident in the thinking of the AAF planners except where it applied directly to the strategic bombing mission. Where Mahan ignored the impact of technology on overland travel, and the effect of rapid overland travel on the importance of sea power, the Air Corps planners neglected to study the changing impact that overland transportation of armies by use of the tank and truck and even the airplane was to have on the relative advantages of the offensive over the defensive in warfare. The parallel between Mahan and his airpower counterparts is striking; the great American naval strategist seems to have provided the theoretical bases for the usurpation by the air force of the primary means of ensuring national security.

A major difference between the airpower enthusiasts and Mahan was that while the latter lived in a period when the British fleet was the largest in the world, the former faced a postwar world situation in which no other state would possess the strategic bombardment capability with which the United States would end the war. The U.S. and Great Britain alone had developed a strategic bombardment capability, and, in the 1943–45 period, the planners foresaw that with the B-29, B-32, and B-36 the United States qualitative and quantitative lead over Great Britain in the postwar world would be appreciable. The AAF planners thus anticipated an enviable situation which in turn presented a dilemma. The dilemma, of course, was the difficulty of justifying a large Air Force when no country in the world presented a real threat to the United States.

Two factors helped them as they looked for justification. First, they anticipated that the impending international organization would have a military force based largely on airpower. Second, the expeditious build-up of airpower within Nazi Germany was indicative of the rapidity with which any industrial state might close the airpower gap through concentration on airpower development. Even taking these two factors into consideration, the planners' case for a large air-force-in-being was weak. The sneak attack on Pearl Harbor presented another case for a strong Air Force, but not necessarily a strategic one.

The arguments for strategic bombardment had evolved from the early 1930's to the period 1943–45. Destruction of enemy fleets on the high seas had been used as a justification for bombers when the range of bombers was short and the dangers from Western Hemisphere states appeared nonexistent. As the United States Navy developed an effective carrier-borne air arm which could effectively intercept and disrupt an invading fleet, the Army Air Forces had difficulty justifying the strategic bombardment mission since even the B-17 did not have the combat radius to reach the heartland of any potential enemy of the middle and late thirties. The possibility of the Axis powers' establishing bases in the Western Hemisphere was used in the late thirties as an argument to warrant the development and expansion of strategic bombardment to destroy these bases before an attack from them could be launched against the United States. The AAF postwar planners had a precedent in assuming that a danger lay in the south, and therefore they planned for a large, deployed force in the Caribbean, with additional bases in South America.

Another fundamental difference between the beliefs of Mahan and AAF planners was that the latter were convinced that the encounter between opposing air forces would not take place within the operating medium (that is, in the air). They believed that victory would go to the state which could destroy first the enemy's offensive and then his defensive air capabilities, to be followed by the demolition of his industries, and the undermining of his will to continue the war.

The doctrine of Douhet, modified by the Tactical School in the thirties and generally accepted throughout AAF Headquarters, had an important effect upon all the postwar AAF plans. Douhet provided the basic military theory of strategic bombardment while Mahan apparently provided some of the political and economic, as well as strategic, bases for the assumptions that would justify the Douhetan approach to national security. The marriage of modified Mahan to modified Douhet provided the doctrinal structure upon which most of the postwar Air Force would be built.

4

International Relations, International Organization, and Potential Enemies

I

The AAF officers who constructed the postwar plans in the 1943–45 period held certain theories of international relations which influenced the assumptions they made and the force structures they held to be necessary. Although opinion was not unanimous and an occasional dissenting voice was heard, the coincidence of conceptual thought makes generalization possible.

The planners believed that conflict and war were inevitable in the world and did not seriously consider any utopian plan for world peace. Their conviction that the United States would be involved in future wars was evident from their references to "the next war." They held a crude cyclical theory of war, being convinced that major wars were generational phenomena, with each major conflict followed by a twenty-year period of peace, abhorrence of violence by all people, and general pacifism among those peoples who had been involved in the previous war.[1] The planners had been influenced by some of the writings of the 1930's and held an economic theory of war causation, based vaguely (and certainly indirectly) on the writings of Lenin. They, naturally, did not consider the possibility that military men and armaments might be causes of tension, conflict, and war. They assumed that any vacuum of power would invite aggression and constructed a justification for preclusive imperialism to prevent such vacuums from occurring.

They measured a state's power by heavily weighting technology and by assigning lesser values to natural resources, manpower, and ideology. They considered maintenance of world peace an important postwar policy goal for the United States and thought that the goal could be accomplished only through enforcement measures. They had considerable faith in the future international organization, for they saw it as a law enforcement body based largely on American military strength and more specifically on American airpower. Their faith grew out of the assumption that the United Nations would be an instrument of American foreign policy, which would be one of world peace through deterrence, if possible, and enforcement, if not. If the United Nations were to fail, as a few planners assumed it would, the tragedy would not be considered a great one, for the United States would carry out its role as the guarantor of peace with or without this organization.

The planners were generally ahistorical and usually theorized from personal experience. The lesson of the League of Nations was that it had failed because the United States was not a member and because it

1. Interviews with Norstad and Giffin.

39

lacked airpower. Conflict and war resulted from "have not" nations seeking to expand and to obtain the *lebensraum* and overseas trade that the "have" nations enjoyed; this conflict and war could be prevented by supplying the needs of the "have not" nations or by enforcement action if those demands proved excessive. Airpower was considered the guarantor of peace for two reasons: its deterrent value and its ability to strike rapidly and decisively against aggressors.

There is no evidence that the AAF planners considered the possibility that airpower was a two-edged sword and that an aggressor nation might possess sufficient airpower to defeat the United Nations or the United States. Implicit was the assumption that the United States would maintain alliances in the postwar world with all the major war allies except the Soviet Union.

The Initial Postwar Air Force Plan (105 groups) was based on a number of assumptions which were drawn from independent thinking of the planners within the Air Staff, Plans. Although this was the first formal plan for the postwar Air Force, an earlier study had been made by Brigadier General O. A. Anderson, who was Assistant Chief of Air Staff, Plans, in April 1943.[2] Entitled *A Study to Determine the Minimum Air Power the United States Should Have at the Conclusion of the War in Europe*, the report was primarily concerned with the minimum airpower needed between V-E and V-J Days, but it also considered postwar airpower needs. Under paragraph 3, Criteria, Anderson wrote:

> Military forces are justified only as necessary means of implementing national policies for the accomplishment of national objectives. A determination of the desired ultimate strength of our air arm therefore hinges upon a discovery and appreciation of our national objectives related in point of time to (1) the signing of the German armistice, and (2) the immediately succeeding period of treaty conferences, and European post-war readjustments. The latter will probably proceed concurrently with the first phase of the war with Japan, unless unforeseen developments alter our present over-all strategic program.[3]

To ascertain these national objectives, which were Anderson's starting points in determining the size and composition of military forces, he surveyed "authoritative utterances of the President and Secretary of State, and senatorial comment, relative to our national objectives, the accomplishment of which will be involved at the time of the armistice terminating the war in Europe, and during the formulation of treaties governing post-war reorganization."[4] These "utterances" appear in

2. 145.96–125; 8092–160. Anderson's position was comparable to that held by Kuter and Norstad. His official title was Assistant Chief of the Air Staff, Operational Plans; this was changed to Assistant Chief of the Air Staff, Plans, in May or June 1943.

3. *Ibid.*, pp. 1–2.

4. *Ibid.*, p. 2.

Tab A to the Anderson study and are used to justify Anderson's five national objectives at V-E Day.

(a) Avoidance of chaos in Europe.
(b) Restoration of sovereign rights and self-government to those who have been forcibly deprived of them.
(c) Establishment of Western Hemisphere solidarity and security, under United States leadership.
(d) Insurance of permanent world peace, and a stabilized world economy, to be achieved by use of an international military force.
(e) Accomplishment of an orderly transition of industrial organization of the United States, and of the world, from a war-time to a peace-time basis.[5]

Keeping these national objectives in mind, Anderson recommended a force of 273 groups with 45,000 tactical airplanes, and indicated that, in addition to the continuation of the war against Japan, the United States would have to face the problem of an expansionistic Russia in Europe.

Unless Great Britain and the United States are in position to join her in doing so, Russia may have sufficient provocation to alone occupy and assume control of not only all of Germany, but all of Central and Eastern Europe, now under Axis domination. Thereafter she might be disposed to amend her recently announced intentions as to territorial expansion.

The strength and mobility of our armed forces (relative to those of our allies) with which we are in position to immediately support our views expressed at the peace table will have much to do with the reception which those views receive.[6]

After giving a number of reasons why he thought that the United States ground forces remaining in Europe would be considerably smaller than those of Russia and Britain, Anderson indicated that the United States should keep sizeable air forces, specifically long-range bombardment aircraft, to "off-set the probably preponderant ground forces of Russia and England in position to influence the situation in Europe."[7]

Anderson also found a need for a sizeable United States commitment to the "international military force," a force which Anderson anticipated would be largely an air force:

To be effective, within reasonable bounds as to aggregate strength, it must be highly mobile. To be highly mobile it must be predominantly an air force, with sufficient surface forces to provide local security and logistic support for international bases, and to temporarily garrison recalcitrant areas. This principal offensive weapon will be the heavy bomber, of medium (present "long range") and long range.[8]

5. *Ibid.*, Tab A, pp. 2–3.   6. *Ibid.*, pp. 3–4.
7. *Ibid.*, p. 5.   8. *Ibid.*, p. 6.

Anderson continued with his concept of an international military force by proposing that the United States should provide 50 per cent of the air component of the international force for Europe and the Western Hemisphere.[9]   Assuming, as he did, that the bulk of the air war against Japan would be fought by United States forces, the airpower requirements to offset Russian ground strength in Europe, to supply 50 per cent of the international air force, and to defeat Japan would be enormous in Anderson's view, and the figure of 273 groups was not incompatible with his assumptions.

Anderson seemed to assume that the international military force in the postwar world would be an instrument of American foreign policy. "Our air forces required for the purposes stated . . . above [prevention of chaos in Europe, retention of military strength to allow negotiation from strength, control of controversial areas, supply of the major portion of the air forces to control Europe, maintenance of Western Hemisphere solidarity and security] should become available to serve our purposes in the establishment of an international armed force; first in the Western Hemisphere and Europe—in Asia and the Pacific after our defeat of Japan."[10] Of all Anderson's assumptions, this one remained almost unmodified during the next two crucial years.   It is important to realize that much of Anderson's thinking in this brief study was the basis for later studies and plans.

When in September 1943 the PWD was directed to produce a plan which would outline the Air Force requirements in the postwar world, the planners had little to guide them.   It is interesting to try to determine how much of the plan was internally developed within the AAF and how much guidance was received from the President, the State Department, and the War Department.   Such guidance came either through JCS/War Department channels or through public pronouncements.   The State Department's influence on the planning was minimal for a number of reasons.   One was that it considered the postwar planning period largely within its own domain.   Attempts by General Tompkins of the War Department's SPD and Colonel Davison of the SPO to get planning guidance from this department were unsuccessful.[11]   A second reason was that rapport between the postwar planners and the State Department was never established formally or informally.   What contact there was from 1943 through 1945 was strained because of the exclusion of the State Department from much of the wartime policymaking, and because of the complex coordination necessary among the War Department's Civil Affairs Division and Operations Division, the Joint Chiefs of Staff and its various committees, and the State Department.[12]

From the War Department came certain basic assumptions: that the war in Europe would come to a successful conclusion about one year

9. *Ibid.*
10. *Ibid.*, pp. 6–7.
11. Interviews with Tompkins and Davison.
12. Interview with Philip E. Mosley.

prior to victory in the Pacific, that partial demobilization might begin with victory in Europe, that the United States would supply some of the emergency interim forces required to maintain order and to guarantee adequate consideration of American peace aims (the aims themselves were not given), that the United States would furnish a share of an international police force, and that some form of universal military training would be maintained in the United States.[13]   The AAF planners also normally received some Joint Chiefs of Staff guidance through the SPD.

Thus, when the creative act of drawing up the initial postwar plan was undertaken in the autumn of 1943, the planners had very broad assumptions with which to work, and only with subsequent plans did budgetary constraints and specific manpower and group limitations restrict their latitude.   The relative freedom to make assumptions, design force levels, and predict base requirements gave the planners an opportunity to evolve a force structure based on anticipated needs for the maintenance of national security in the kind of world that they foresaw when hostilities ceased.   If the War Department had designed a structure prior to late 1943 and told the AAF planners to live within the boundaries established by such a plan, the planners would have lost their opportunity to be creative.

2

Prior to the formation of the PWD some specific consideration had been given to the ramifications of an international organization for the maintenance of peace and security as well as to the size and purposes of an international police force.   The Joint Chiefs of Staff perceived a need in January 1943 for some study concerning air-base requirements for an international police force and requested one of its committees, the Joint Staff Planners, to undertake such a study to determine "Where it is desired that International Police Force air facilities be located throughout the world, this plan to be without regard to current sovereignty."[14] The JPS subcommittee, finding no precedent to give it guidance on the "political and international implications of an International Police Force,"[15] decided to base its planning for the air facilities that would be required for the force on a number of hypotheses.

Thus, the desire on the part of the JCS to determine what air bases might be needed by a postwar international organization inspired the first military thinking on what this organization should be expected to accomplish, how it might accomplish its goals, and what military forces

13. Memorandum from Special Planning Division of the War Department Special Staff to the Joint Chiefs of Staff, 30 July 1943 (assumptions in enclosure B to this memorandum).   145.86–53; 4334–133.

14. Notes on conference between [*sic*] Captain Haskins, U.S.N., Colonel Harris, Army Air Forces, and Colonel Wolfinbarger, War Department General Staff (25 January 1943), p. 1.   145.86–15; 4334–55.   These three officers were the members of this subcommittee: Captain Haskins was soon replaced by Captain Gardner, U.S.N., and Lieutenant Colonel Joseph Halverson was an alternate AAF member.

15. *Ibid.*

it might require. The original Joint Staff Planners' directive to its subcommittee was restricted to air-base requirements and did not request a study of naval and army base needs or the other problems which would have to be considered in the establishment of an international police force: force levels, organization of military forces, contributions of military forces by various states, training, command, and financing.[16]

The basic assumptions adopted for consideration at the next meeting of the committee are as follows:

1. The essential nature of any Post War I.P.F. will be based on the application of Air Power, and such a force will be essentially an Air Force.

2. The employment of a force, based on the Application of Air Power, must have ground installations and facilities, generally along the Strategic Air Routes of the World.

3. An International Police Force will be employed as its name suggests. That is, not as an army to wage war after a situation has gotten out of control, but as a force which will eliminate subversive or dangerous focal points before they can develop to the point where they become a danger to the security of the world.[17]

The narrow mandate under which the committee operated apparently restricted the assumptions it could make, but its meetings did inspire the planners to consider seriously some of the ramifications of an international police force. The early planning reveals some insights into military concepts of international organizations and more specifically into AAF ideas concerning international police forces.

The AAF planners on this subcommittee envisioned an international police force composed largely of air forces, conceived as having "as their principal weapon a striking force of heavy bombardment aircraft with adequate fighter protection and transport facilities."[18] Lieutenant Colonel Joseph Halverson from the Air Staff, Plans, expanded somewhat on the specific suppositions made by the subcommittee, of which he was an alternate member. He indicated that the goals of the international organization would be identical to those of American foreign policy, and that potential enemies of the United States would be those states posing threats to world peace.

The following factors ... should be considered with respect to actual location of bases:

a. Locations with respect to our future potential enemies who may have the capability to wage war.

Colonel Halverson's numerous references to the threats to the peace as "our enemies" indicate that he equated United States national security threats with threats to the international organization.[19]

16. *Ibid.*
17. *Ibid.*, p. 2.
18. Halverson's comments on the second meeting of the JPS subcommittee (26 January 1943), p. 1.   145.86–15; 4334–55.
19. *Ibid.*

The favorable attitude of the AAF planners toward the future international organization was based on three hypotheses: that the enforcement machinery would be largely air forces; that the United States contribution to this international air force would be substantial; and that the international organization would be used by the United States as an extension of American foreign policy in helping to identify and deter potential enemies of the United States. A few days after the initial concept of an international police force based largely on airpower was tentatively agreed upon by this JPS subcommittee studying "Air Facilities for International Police Force," Captain Gardner, the senior United States Navy member, took issue with the role of airpower. On 29 January 1943 he requested a recess of the subcommittee due to lack of "factual data" from which the subcommittee might draw its hypotheses and determine the air-facility requirements for the international police force.[20]   Within the next two weeks the United States Navy had managed to have this study cancelled and to have the Joint Strategic Survey Committee undertake a broader study which would consider Navy as well as Air Force base needs for the postwar world.[21]   The result of this action was to remove from the postwar planners any direct contact with the overseas base planning of the Joint Chiefs of Staff.

From a study undertaken to determine tentative air-facility requirements for an international police force there evolved, under the stimulus of interservice competition, the first serious consideration by Navy and AAF planners alike of postwar overseas base requirements for the United States.   For a brief period in early 1943 an attempt was made by the AAF planners to estimate what an international organization might accomplish in the postwar world and what role the United States Air Force might play within the enforcement machinery of such an organization.

From February 1943 until early 1945 little further consideration was given to international organization or international police forces, although each plan drawn up did incorporate the concepts developed in January 1943: that there would be such an organization, that airpower would be the dominant force within the international police force, and that the United States contribution to this force would be substantial.   The AAF planners' attitude toward a postwar international organization was ambivalent.   There seemed to be no great affection for the idea on the part of some planners, nor much faith that a workable international peacekeeping system could be established.

20. Memorandum for General Anderson.   Subject: JPS Subcommittee studying "Air Facilities for International Police Force," from Colonel Joseph Halverson (17 February 1943), p. 1.
21. *Ibid*. The Joint Strategic Survey Committee was a committee of the Joint Chiefs of Staff which made recommendations on "global and theater strategy."   Its members were Lieutenant General Stanley D. Embrick, U.S. Army, Major General Muir S. Fairchild, AAF, Vice Admiral Russell Willson, U.S. Navy.   Maurice Matloff, *Strategic Planning for Coalition Warfare: 1943–1944*, p. 108.

45

In considering the location of . . . bases for the International Police Force, two somewhat conflicting factors must be kept in mind:

a. They should be so strategically placed as to permit the earliest possible application of force upon any incipient disturber of world peace.

b. The more efficiently located, the more surely they constitute a potential threat against the purely nationalistic security of adjacent territories.

This latter argument is strong enough to raise a grave question whether the theory of an International Police Force and any idea of individual national defense are not mutually exclusive.[22]

Therefore, all planning from the spring of 1943 until early 1945 allowed for the contingency of either an ineffective international organization for the maintenance of peace or for an effective one. There seemed to be no normative aspect in AAF planning since *no* international organization would mean a larger national air force, while an *effective* organization would entail a smaller force but would also require a large U.S. contingent to be assigned or attached to it.

In January 1945 a draft of a proposed statement of policy was circulated for coordination among the AAF sections. The statement, entitled "The Peacetime Mission and Functions of the Army Air Forces," mentioned that the AAF would have two principal functions:

FIRST, to maintain in a continuing state of readiness to act, a force of such offensive and defensive power that its mere existence should deter any lawless aggression. This force must be capable of immediate action to forestall any armed threat to this country before it gains momentum and if necessary of continuing full scale operations. It must in addition be capable of carrying out any responsibilities assumed by the United States for combined international peace enforcement action, either by furnishing U.S. Air Force contingents or by other action against threats to world peace and security.

SECOND, in conjunction with land and naval forces to provide air forces required for the conduct of combined operations.[23]

General Harold George, Commander of Air Transport Command, and an important figure in the development of Air Corps doctrine in the Tactical School at Maxwell AFB in the middle thirties, noted an inconsistency in the first two sentences of the first function. Two deterrent force levels seemed to be required, one to prevent any lawless aggression, and the other to forestall an armed threat to this country, the latter being the smaller. Arnold's Advisory Council was unable to grasp the

22. Memorandum from Commanding General, United States Army Air Forces to Joint Chiefs of Staff. Subject: United States Military Requirements for Territories (2 November 1943). Inclosure A, pp. 3–4. 145.86–67; 4334-161. This memorandum was written by the PWD (author unknown).

23. (8 January 1945), p. 1. 145.86–69B; 2–2141–26. Written by the PWD (author unknown).

meaning of General George's question and left the wording as it stood. In the words of the Advisory Council,

> General George concurred in [*sic*] the paper with one exception, that in the final section under paragraph 3 wherein it states:
> "A force of such offensive and defensive power that its mere existence should deter any lawless aggression." General George stated that he thought there was a great difference between this and a course which would deter any aggression "against the U.S." As it was presented to General Arnold, the Advisory Council does not believe the change suggested by General George was desirable.[24]

The Post War Division, like the Advisory Council, was unable to grasp the difference between national defense and prevention of all aggression.

> The history of military appropriations casts a dark shadow over current postwar planning. It is inevitable that postwar legislation will grant appropriations to governmental agencies in direct proportions to their respective political force.
>
> The basic problem revolves into the steps necessary for the non-political Air Force to obtain the political force necessary to obtain the essential appropriations.
>
> The time element for this publicity and liaison work is critical. It should start immediately in order that the principle of a continuous strong international defense, represented by a large air force, will be doctrine in all postwar legislative and executive planning.[25]

If a force large enough to deter any lawless aggression was to be provided by the United States, why was an international force necessary? The explanation seems to be that the United States would keep the peace in the postwar world either through unilateral action or through an international organization which would have a force composed largely of United States air forces. The AAF planners seemed to have no preference between these two systems, except that their awareness of the need for overseas bases made the international peace force seem attractive, since in their view an international organization could be less concerned about sovereignty than the United States would have to be.[26] In addition, an international police force with a large United States contingent would serve as a justification for the deployment of United States military forces of greater size than those needed for national defense, since the planners assumed that the United States would need a national defense force in addition to its contribution to the international police force.

24. Attachment to policy statement of 8 January 1945. 145.86–69B.

25. Moffat to Norstad (4 July 1945), p. 1. The phrase "international defense" was not defined but appears to be something more than national defense.

26. Memorandum. Subject: United States Military Requirements.... Inclosure A (2 November 1943), p. 4.

The AAF planners did not regard the United Nations as a threat to United States sovereignty, to her national military force, postwar position, military airpower, or to any of their other values. They assumed that the efficacy of an international organization would be greatly increased if it had a large airpower capability. There is no evidence that the AAF ever attempted to analyze the reasons for the failure of the League of Nations; the concept of collective security against an aggressor was accepted as a valid basis for an international peacekeeping organization, especially since the planners assumed that United States airpower in the service of the international organization would doom any aggressive action from any power, large or small.

The postwar planners devised a scheme for designating two types of bases.

> Type A—Those essential and exclusive to the defense of the United States, our territories and the Western Hemisphere. Type B—Those essential to the functioning of an International Police Force.

> While distinct, these categories are inter-related since a "B" base could in emergency serve as an "A" base, provided the U.S. rights to it and our ability to defend it were sufficient to interdict its use to others when our national interest so dictated.[27]

There seems to be little doubt that if the international organization was looked upon with any favor by the postwar planners it was not out of any great faith in collective security but out of a desire to justify a large postwar United States Air Force with world-wide base facilities.

There was a consensus among the planners and leaders of the AAF that airpower had certain qualities that would make it the primary means for maintaining postwar peace. This was usually accepted as a given, and detailed consideration of how airpower would accomplish this goal was not undertaken.[28] The AAF doctrine that airpower was decisive in warfare was combined with a theory of deterrence whereby a large, ready air force could not only defeat an aggressor but deter a potential aggressor from taking this action; this was easily transformed by the postwar planners into the concept of an international police force. In Colonel Halverson's words: "An International Police Force will be employed as its name suggests. That is; not as an army to wage war after a situation has gotten [sic] out of control, but as a force which will eliminate subversive or dangerous focal points before they can develop to the point where they become a danger to the security of the world."[29]

The postwar planners consistently argued for a large, ready force,

27. *Ibid.*
28. "Present developments in warfare indicate that air power will be the most effective and the most economical instrument for maintaining peace and enforcing the decisions of whatever form of world organization emerges from the peace settlements." Letter from General Stratemeyer, Commanding General, 10th Air Force, China-Burma-India Theater, to General Arnold (30 August 1944). 168.491; 3–8711.
29. Halverson's comments on second meeting of JPS subcommittee (26 January 1943), p. 2.

deployed to strategic bases and ready to act instantly to resist aggression. To justify this force, the planners emphasized the increased danger of surprise attacks as well as the increased danger of assuming that time would be available to mobilize an air force. With the reasons submitted for a ready air force came a theory of deterrence which would have increasing importance in the postwar era.

> ... the "READY" force has the unique characteristic of being a force that *prevents* the launching of an enemy attack. It does this in two ways. First, because it can pass over all obstacles and be brought to bear quickly in the precise spot where an enemy attack is being mounted, it can snuff out the enemy threat before it is launched. Second, its very existence acts as a deterrent.[30]

The planners, feeling threatened by the War Department concept of mobilization, hinted, in making their case for deterrent forces, at a willingness to launch pre-emptive attacks against an aggressor. For example, the passage quoted above contains the assurance that " . . . it [the force] can snuff out the enemy threat before it is launched." The planners were aware that theories of deterrence in an era of advanced technology presented one difficulty of particular importance: What if deterrence were to fail? They were willing to launch a pre-emptive attack against an enemy about to strike; they did not pursue the problems of determining at what point such an attack could be presumed inevitable, thereby warranting a pre-emptive attack, or how the concept of pre-emptive attack could be made acceptable to the American attitude on aggressive war. An international police force would solve these problems fairly well, for if the international organization decided that a certain nation was an immediate threat to peace it could launch a pre-emptive attack without being called an aggressor. The organization as an instrument of American foreign policy presented to the postwar planners a useful means, otherwise unavailable, for carrying out desired policy. The concepts of deterrence and pre-emptive attack, combined with the instrument of an international police force, gave the planners the practical justification they needed for a large, ready Air Force and the moral justification for its use.

The planners were an extremely optimistic group, probably because they were convinced that American airpower was winning World War II. The enormous role that the Russians, the British, and the Chinese, as well as the United States Navy, Marines, and Army were playing in the victory was not recognized by the Air Force planners. Conflict and war, they felt, would always occur, but wars would be brought quickly to an end through American airpower, assuming that the American people were willing to maintain a large regular force.

There was considerable disappointment among those AAF leaders directly concerned with negotiations for the international organization

---

30. "4th Draft of Plans for the Post-War Air Force: Outlines for General Norstad," authored by Colonel Phillip Cole, one of Colonel Moffat's assistants in the PWD (1 May 1945), p. 2.

when the veto limited the collective security aspects of the United Nations. Major General Muir Fairchild, the senior AAF officer concerned, when discussing his personal reaction to the decision to have a veto on the substantive issues in the Security Council, was quoted as saying, "Something inside me died." [31] The need for a sizeable international police force with a preponderant United States airpower commitment was lost with the decision to require unanimity on substantive matters among the five permanent members of the Security Council of the proposed United Nations. The disappointment among AAF leaders was twofold: the organization envisaged by them from 1943 until early 1945 was to have been one that would maintain peace among all states and not just among the smaller nations; the requirements for such a limited international police force would be so small that the AAF case for large forces in support of it was lost when the Yalta decisions were made. In fact, the reaction of the planners to the veto was that an international police force was probably unnecessary, as is indicated by this quote from a Strategy Division study: "It is hard to imagine a situation where a direct order of the Security Council, followed by such disturbing measures as complete or partial interruption of economic relations and rail, sea, air, postal, telegraphic, radio, and other means of communications, and the severance of diplomatic relations, would not be enough to bring any minor power to its senses." [32] Therefore, the enthusiasm for the international organization shown by some AAF leaders and planners was for what they had assumed would be a collective security organization with large military forces assigned to an international police force (or United States forces earmarked for use by the international organization). Although the planners from the Strategy Division (the Air Staff, Plans) recognized that the United Nations charter did not conform to the AAF 1943 conception of the postwar international organization, the Post War Division was generally unaware of the meaning of the decisions taken at Yalta and at San Francisco. In May 1945, Colonel Cole of the PWD indicated that "international policing" under the auspices of the United Nations could handle the following situations:

a. Threat of renewed military activity on a major scale by the defeated enemy states.

b. Clear aggression by a small state against a neighbor.

c. Border conflict, with initial responsibility for aggression not immediately apparent, between small states.

d. Aggression or intervention by one of the major United Nations against a weaker nation (a neighbor).

e. Attack by one of the major United Nations upon another.

f. Conflict between two of the major United Nations in which the placing of the responsibility is not immediately and unquestionably clear. [33]

31. Smart interview.
32. Study by Strategy Division, Air Staff, Plans (31 July 1945), p. 4.
33. "USAAF Participation in an International Air Force," 2d Draft (1 May 1945), pp. 2–3.   145.86–95; 2–2141–37.

Also in May, the Permanent Establishment Branch of the PWD estimated that the "Initial complement of World Security Organization" would be 75 groups and 40 separate squadrons;[34] this figure so closely approximated the figures of 78 groups for the interim U.S. Air Force and the 75 groups for the permanent Air Force (which were the approved AAF figures at this same time—May 1945) that it seems evident that the PWD still conceived of the United Nations as an international police force charged to keep the peace among the great powers as well as the small. A force of this size (75 groups) for the international police force was considerably in excess of what would be required to deter aggression by a minor power; since it was approximately the size of the anticipated United States postwar air force and since that air force was assumed to be large enough to deter any lawless aggression, there can be little doubt that the PWD failed to understand the very limited goals incorporated in the United Nations charter.

The postwar planners saw no good reason to restrict the scope of the future organization to conflicts among smaller states when American U.N. airpower could maintain the peace against all states, large or small. The postwar planners envisioned the international organization as a kind of rudimentary world government, dominated by the United States and relying on American airpower for its enforcement and deterrent functions. The international organization devised at the Dumbarton Oaks, Yalta, and San Francisco conferences differed greatly from this AAF concept, yet the Post War Division was totally unaware until May 1945, or later, that the United Nations would neither be an American controlled world government nor require large contingents of United States air forces. The enthusiasm for the international organization displayed by many planners was based not only on their desire to obtain overseas bases and to justify a large postwar air force but also on a misconception of the role and scope of the United Nations.

3

Despite General Anderson's concern about the dangers of the Soviet Union in the postwar world, the planners viewed a resurgent Japan or Germany as the probable immediate enemy, with the Soviet Union providing the long-term threat, commencing no earlier than twenty years after the end of World War II. Japan and Germany were regarded as the greatest threats because both had exhibited the technological ability to use airpower offensively. Having identified the two potential enemies, the planners then eliminated Germany as a threat to American national security since it was assumed that Britain and the Soviet Union could contain that threat. Although there was certainly some concern about the long-term danger presented by the Soviet Union, it was based largely on distrust of the Soviet leaders which grew out of the constant difficulties

34. Memorandum for Record. Subject: International Air Force (11 May 1945), Chart B. 145.86–95; 2–2141–37.

encountered by various AAF personnel in their dealings with the Russians.[35]

The Air Force planners viewed threats to national security largely in terms of technology as it related to airpower. If airpower was the key to national security and national strength, no other state would pose a threat unless it possessed a sophisticated air force. If, in turn, the key to airpower was the strategic offensive, then no state could be a threat without large numbers of aircraft with a strategic capability. Since in 1944 the Soviet Union neither possessed a long-range bomber nor accepted the doctrine of strategic bombardment, it could not be an immediate postwar danger to the United States. Thus, whenever a study mentioned Russia as a major postwar threat, the danger was never considered immediate. Discussion about the primitive nature of Soviet aviation technology was usually based on Russian performance in World War II. Little consideration was given to the doctrinal factors that led the Soviets to fighter and light-bomber development, or to the immediate problems of defense which diverted them from bomber development. It was assumed that deficiencies in technological sophistication were the reason the Soviets did not develop a strategic air capability in World War II.

The AAF had more contact with the Soviets prior to May 1945 than did the other U.S. military services. The *Frantic* operation involving shuttle bombing, whereby the United States bombers on missions into Eastern Germany would recover at Poltava and other Russian bases, had given Spaatz, Eaker, and many less senior officers first-hand experience with the intransigence of the political leadership in Russia. The problems encountered in connection with lend-lease aircraft in the Alaska-to-Siberia pipeline had caused the AAF leaders to entertain serious doubts about postwar cooperation with the Soviet Union. The problems involved with the release of AAF pilots who had landed behind Russian lines, the difficulties of coordination with Russian military officials with regard to the position of Soviet front-line troops (one incident resulting in an American aircraft strafing Russian troops and killing a Russian lieutenant general),[36] the breakdown in negotiations over *Frantic* bases for AAF fighter aircraft in the Balkans, all contributed to the uneasiness of AAF officers familiar with these and other incidents.[37] The opinion was widespread among AAF leaders that since the Russians were difficult to deal with when closely allied with the United States in a military effort against a common enemy, the relationship would become even more difficult once that enemy had been defeated. The AAF planners were aware that throughout the war AAF leaders had refused to give long-range bombers to the Soviet Union.

35. Interviews with Kuter, Cabell, and Hansell.
36. Letter from Eaker to Arnold (21 November 1944). 168.491; 3–4711–5.
37. The file of Arnold's communication with the major AAF commanders contains much information on the continuing difficulties encountered in dealing with the Russians, especially the Eaker and Spaatz portions of that file. 168.491.

Yet these factors had little impact on postwar planning for two reasons: as has been stated, the Russians did not seem to present an immediate threat; and second, the strategic bombardment doctrine was not applicable in the case of Russia. Since the mid-1930's, the AAF strategic doctrine had been based on the conviction that any enemy could be forced to surrender, even without ground attack, through rationally applied strategic bombardment. Yet Russia presented a difficult question: Could a vast continental state with dispersed industry and agriculture be defeated through airpower alone? Hitler, who had managed to capture almost half the industrial and agricultural resources of the Soviet Union, was still unable to force a Soviet surrender. Russia was thus a very probable exception to the AAF doctrine. The Navy, during this same period, was also eliminating Russia as a potential enemy—because it had no fleet.[38]

Thus, Germany and Japan continued to be considered the potential enemies—because both were technologically equipped to construct strategic air forces, and because both had the concentration of industry, population, and communication systems that could neatly be destroyed by strategic bombardment. The Air Force moved from a preferred strategy, strategic bombardment, to preferred enemies, Japan and Germany, who would, in turn, fit the preferred strategy. And the resurgence of these two erstwhile enemies was easy to envision—hadn't the Germany of the thirties demonstrated a fearsome ability not only to recover from defeat but to go forward with even greater strength and vigor?

There seems to be little evidence that the planners appreciated the decline in the security position of the United States that was taking place throughout the planning period as a result of revolutionary technological developments and the collapse of the European balance of power.[39] Potential enemies were selected not because of the danger they actually presented to American national security but rather as they followed the pattern of past military enemy identification.

38. Vincent Davis, *Postwar Defense Policy and the U.S. Navy, 1943–1946* (Chapel Hill: University of North Carolina Press, 1966), p. 18.

39. "The American security position following World War II was undermined by two concurrent developments: the collapse of the European balance of power and the advent of nuclear weapons systems." Warner R. Schilling, Paul Y. Hammond, and Glenn H. Snyder, *Strategy, Politics, and Defense Budgets* (New York: Columbia University Press, 1962), p. 8.

5

The Evolution of Force Structures

The Army Air Force (from August 1945 to September 1947) and the United States Air Force (from September 1947 until the initiation of the Korean War) maintained a position that seventy air groups were necessary to ensure the national security of the United States. There has been considerable perplexity among students of this period as to how the 70-group figure was reached. Although basically an arbitrary figure, it was reached only after two years of extensive planning, coordination, bargaining, and discussion among the Post War Division, the Air Staff, Plans, and other agencies within and without the Air Staff.[1] The 70-group plan, the fifth major plan produced by the postwar planners, was to become the most important. The four previous plans must be studied in order to understand fully both the 70-group plan and the assumptions on which it was based. This is necessary since the 70-group figure was not reached by drawing up a formal plan, and because the factors and discussions leading up to it have, until now, been buried in the files of the Army Air Force. Therefore, the annals must begin with the Initial Postwar Plan (105 groups), the planning inputs leading up to that plan, and the various factors that led to the gradual diminishment of the 105-group figure of July 1943 to the 70-group figure of August 1945.[2]

General Arnold's desire for an autonomous Air Force in the postwar period and his recognition of the necessity of planning in wartime for that objective, Kuter's realization of the continuing need for long-range planning, and the flow of queries from numerous agencies requesting information about AAF postwar requirements all contributed to the pressure on the AAF to produce a postwar plan. A well thought out and coordinated plan would give the Air Force the ammunition it needed to face Congress, the War Department, and the press with a unified position on autonomy, overseas bases, group requirements, Universal Military Training, AAA, and a myriad of other requirements and issues that could be anticipated as areas of debate or dispute in the immediate postwar period.

The only guidance received from the War Department as to specific numbers of groups came in a memorandum from Major General Thomas

1. "... the Air Force never explained the strategic calculations on which its requested force levels were based." Walter Millis with Harvey C. Mansfield and Harold Stein, *Arms and the State: Civil-Military Elements in National Policy* (New York: Twentieth Century Fund, 1958), p. 148.

2. For a discussion of the omnipresence of the 70-group figure in Air Force planning from 1945 to 1950, see Samuel P. Huntington, *The Common Defense: Strategic Programs in National Politics* (New York: Columbia University Press, 1961), pp. 375 ff.

T. Handy, Assistant Chief of Staff, to General Marshall on 29 July 1943, which indicated that:

> ... a reasonable estimate of the *Interim Forces* on a date six months after the defeat of Japan and eighteen months after the defeat of Germany, would be approximately 1,571,500 men. They will be deployed as follows: European Theater (8 divs, 30 air groups) 379,000, Pacific Theater (11 divs, 25 air groups) 467,500, Continental U.S. and possessions including garrison and overhead (9 divs, 50 air groups) 725,000.[3]

Brigadier General Tompkins, Director of the SPD, incorporated these figures into a memorandum to his chiefs of branches on 5 August.[4] On 7 August 1943, Colonel F. Trubee Davison, Chief of the AAF Special Projects Office, sent to the Assistant Chief of Air Staff, Plans, these memoranda and asked Plans to ". . . determine the balance between class of group which will be required for a. the defeat of Japan and the garrisoning of Europe [and] b. The garrisoning of the world after the defeat of Japan."[5] The 105-group figure was not a hard and fast one but to exceed it would demand that the AAF ". . . defend the requirement for the additional groups."[6] Handy's memorandum had not given any indication as to how the 1,571,500 men would be divided between ground and air forces. Handy stated that there would be 28 divisions and 105 groups, but since the size of wartime divisions and groups varied enormously depending on the mission, there were many ways to divide up and assign these men. The AAF leadership and the PWD accepted the guidance given by General Handy concerning the number of postwar groups (105). Why they accepted this figure with no apparent questioning is not known, but both the close relationship between Marshall and Handy and the large number of groups suggested by the latter may have influenced their decision to approve such a generous figure. The total group strength during the war reached 243 in early 1945, but that of the 1930's never exceeded 30, and the number of operational groups averaged about 15. It should be noted that Handy's figure of 105 groups was an estimate for interim forces; by the spring of 1944 the AAF planners were using the 105-group figure as the basis not only for the immediate postwar period but also for an indefinite time in the future.

A meeting of planners from the various divisions of the Air Staff, Plans, and the Special Projects Office on 13 August 1943 illustrated the dilemma the AAF planners faced as they attempted to decide on the size, composition, and deployment of the postwar Air Force, taking into consideration commercial requirements, the international police force, and United States national security.[7] The purpose of the meeting was

3. 145.86–53; 4334–133.   4. *Ibid.*
5. *Ibid.*   6. *Ibid.*
7. Meeting attended by Colonel F. G. Allen (presiding), Colonel P. M. Hamilton (Chief, Post War Division), Colonel J. G. Hopkins, Colonel Miller (Special Projects Office), Major E. F. Leland (13 August 1943). 168.80–1; 5–2405–4. Colonel Allen, Kuter's personal representative, led the discussion. Kuter was unable to be there since he was attending the Quadrant Conference in Quebec.

to give some broad policy guidance to Colonel Hamilton as he commenced the task of drawing up the first AAF postwar plan.   With the exception of Colonel Hamilton and Colonel Miller there is no evidence that the officers at this meeting contributed anything further to the postwar planning process, but what was said at the meeting did have some important effects on the plans set up during the 1943–45 period.

Colonel Allen understood the dilemma of trying to produce a plan with little guidance from agencies outside the AAF.   "The deployment of the post-war Air Force is contingent upon the foreign policy of the United States.   At this time if we decide on a desired deployment, that in a way will tend to dictate the requirements of our foreign policy."[8]   The others present agreed that there was a dilemma but pointed out that many offices within the AAF, General Arnold, and the SPD were anxious to have a plan formulated as early as possible.   Allen decided that considering these demands (Arnold's desire to have a plan to take to the JCS was the most pressing reason for going ahead as far as Hamilton and Allen were concerned), the AAF Plans officers would have to make certain assumptions and then work from them.

Colonel Allen proceeded to make the various assumptions and gave guidance to the officers present in order to give them some basis for constructing the plan.

> I think that they [the Air Forces] have to be deployed in accordance with an assumed foreign policy and we are going to have to assume that the United States, England, Russia and China—the Big Four that are fighting this war—are going to ally themselves in a post-war alliance for the protection of our mutual interests through the world and in order to preserve peace.[9]

Allen divided the world into "strategic spheres," allotting the United States exclusive "strategic interests" in the Western Hemisphere and the Central Pacific.   Africa was to be a shared strategic interest of England and the United States; the Western Pacific, of China, the United States, and Russia; the South and Southwest Pacific, of the United States and England.   The rest of the world was divided up as follows: Europe, the Middle East, and India—England and Russia; Southeast Asia—China and England.[10]   "Now in these strategic areas in the world wherever the U.S. maintains an interest, it appears to me that we also would maintain Air Force units and I think that can serve as a guide in formulating the plan for the composition of the post-war Air Force."[11]

Allen guided the planners in another area which was later largely neglected by the AAF planners:

> Another thing in studying the strategic aspects of the post-war Air Force, I strongly recommend using this Polar projection of the world as your

8. *Ibid.*, p. 6.   9. *Ibid.*, pp. 6–7.
10. *Ibid.*, p. 8.   11. Allen comment, in *ibid.*

basic map rather than anything else.   Another thing, the areas of power
of the world are relatively few.   There are only three big power areas—
one is the United States—the other is Central and Eastern Europe—and
the other is the China-India area.   On a Polar projection these areas form
a triangle and in the world of the future, I believe that a great deal of air
commerce will be directed between the corners of this triangle.   That
will have to be considered with the access of bases in the vicinity of these
areas.

The war seems to start over who is going to control these areas of power.
Another thing that should be considered in the solution is the pattern of
the ocean trade lines because even in the era of air power the bulk of
commerce will move by the ocean trade lines because it is the cheapest.
We must not only protect those lines but control them.[12]

Thus Allen gave the men who would construct the first AAF plan for the
postwar world some points of departure.   The assumptions specifically
stated in the Initial Post War Air Force plan have a direct correlation
to Colonel Allen's points, and the impact of his thinking is evident
throughout the plan even though there is no evidence that he participated
in its authorship.[13]

Colonel Hamilton thus commenced the task of writing a plan with
General Anderson's study, general War Department guidelines, and
Colonel Allen's guidance—all inputs from offices or individuals outside
the PWD.   The plan went through a number of rough drafts, was
coordinated within the AAF staff, and was eventually produced in
final form on 14 February 1944.   Incorporated within this plan were
the War Department's recommendation of 105 groups as well as
certain assumptions, Allen's comments on assumptions, and Anderson's
advocacy of a postwar air force heavily weighted toward the strategic
mission.

This plan was entitled *Initial Postwar Air Force: Preliminary
Study by Assistant Chief of Air Staff, Plans* (the 105-group plan).[14]
The plan called for 105 groups and 1,000,000 men on active duty; the

---

12. *Ibid.*   (The lack of paragraph indentation is in the original.)
13. The wording of the assumptions of the 105-group plan was as follows (pp. 1–2):
II. *Assumptions.*   2. It is assumed:
   a. That upon cessation of hostilities and establishment of peace, the Nation
will require a permanent military establishment capable of:
   (1) Defending the Western Hemisphere and our possessions.
   (2) Occupying strategic bases for our military defense and our economic
well-being in order to:
   (a) Ensure access to essential raw materials.
   (b) Safeguard our unhampered use of sea routes, and
   (c) Provide for the military protection of our future global air commerce.
   (3) Supplying such international obligations as the United States may
assume in furtherance of a peaceful world order.
   (4) Expanding rapidly into an up-to-date, well-trained, well-equipped force
of highest military quality.
14. 145.041A; 2–2141–61.

balance of bomber, attack, fighter, and transport groups reflected the current AAF doctrine of emphasis on strategic bombardment. Included in this 105-group structure was the Anti-Aircraft Artillery, since Arnold, Kuter, and Oldfield, Arnold's special assistant for AAA, all felt that it should be under Air Force direction and control.[15] The 105 groups were divided as follows: 40 very heavy bombardment groups, 2 heavy bomber groups, 4 medium and light bombardment groups, 45 fighter groups, 3 reconnaissance groups, and 11 troop-carrier groups. On the surface this breakdown seemed to give the strategic bombardment mission only 42 of the 105 groups, or 40 per cent of the total group force, but the need for fighter escort of strategic bombardment aircraft had not only become clear to AAF leaders, but, by the autumn of 1943, even the most avid advocate of strategic bombardment was willing to admit that the beliefs held in the 1930's as to the invulnerability of bombers in formation to fighter attack were no longer valid.[16] Hence the 45 fighter groups must be considered strategic weapons in the sense that their main purpose was the escort of strategic bombers in order to protect them from enemy fighter attacks. Forty-two groups of long-range bombers in addition to 45 groups of long-range fighters gave 87 of the 105 groups to the strategic mission. In addition, the transport groups which were to supply the various bases with personnel, mail, materiel, and strategic materials, were to have a support function which would relate, at least partially, to the strategic mission.[17]

Both Handy and Anderson had suggested sizeable air forces in the European area while Allen had mentioned Europe as an area in which Russia and England shared "strategic interests." The PWD accepted the guidance of Anderson and Handy and allocated 21 groups to the "Atlantic-European Areas."[18] This figure was nine less than Handy had suggested, but 21 groups was still 20 per cent of the anticipated postwar combat strength of the Air Force. The problem of overseas bases in Europe was a continual one for the planners; the PWD throughout the entire period was reluctant to plan for any permanent United States air bases in Europe or Africa. Iceland, the Azores, Liberia, Newfoundland, and Ascension Island were mentioned in later studies as possible base locations, but the PWD never contemplated having U.S. bases in Europe after the temporary occupation period. Although the 105-group plan

---

15. *Ibid.*

16. The most detailed study of the slow realization of the need for long-range escort fighters among the Army Air Force leaders is Bernard Boylan's *Development of the Long-Range Escort Fighter* (Maxwell Air Force Base, Montgomery, Ala.: USAF Historical Study No. 136, 1955). See also Wesley F. Craven and James L. Cate, *The Army Air Forces in World War II* (Chicago: University of Chicago Press, 1949), vol. II, esp. chaps. 20 and 21; Martin Caidin, *Black Thursday* (New York: E. P. Dutton, 1960); William R. Emerson, *Operation Pointblank: A Tale of Bombers and Fighters*, United States Air Force Academy, Harmon Memorial Lectures in Military History, No. 4, 1962.

17. The 105-group plan.

18. *Ibid.*, p. 6.

of 14 February 1944 did not mention bases either in the United States or overseas, the 21-group figure was probably based on the shortage of permanent air bases in the Atlantic area, with 21 groups being the maximum number that could be stationed there.[19]

The total size of the active military forces was assumed to be 2,000,000, with 500,000 for the Army, 500,000 for the Navy, and 1,000,000 for the Air Force.[20] The recommendation received from General Handy was for a total Army and Air Force size of 1,571,500. This total personnel allocation was neatly divided by the AAF planners into approximately 1,000,000 for the Air Force and the remainder, something in excess of 500,000, for the Army. Since the Air Force was considered by the planners to be the primary defense force, the Army and Navy were to handle secondary missions which required smaller forces-in-being. Hence, the proposed Navy size was 500,000 also.[21] Working from a principal assumption that "a strong 'M' day Air Force, strategically deployed for prompt action, will be the most effective insurance against a new outbreak of hostilities in areas within range of its bases," two secondary assumptions followed immediately: "That a land force will be required capable, in cooperation with the other arms, of defending our strategic outpost stations and home bases. . . . That a naval force will be required to assist in the air and land force missions and to safeguard our essential sea lanes from naval attack."[22]

The authors of this plan showed ambivalence over the role of naval aviation. In addition to the assumption quoted above, a number of statements about naval aviation were made. Under "Assumptions" the planners made these suppositions: "That the Air Force will include all military aviation except ship-borne units operating with the Navy, and those artillery-control and 'liaison' units operating with the Army."[23] Under "Discussion," a different approach was taken.

> Size, composition and deployment of the Air Force. Pending a later determination of specific details of the Air Force post war mission and of the precise amount of force and the best order of deployment to accomplish that mission, for present planning purposes it is accepted: That there will exist a "Naval Air Arm" consisting of Air Force trained personnel assigned to the Navy for special training and operations with ship-borne aircraft.[24]

Another statement, concerning naval aviation, was made under "Recommendations": "It is recommended: That specific study be directed in respect to the following problems: Determination of the exact relationship

---

19. The deployment plan which included overseas bases and allocation of groups to these bases was a supplement to the 105-group plan; it was not completed until 14 June 1944. "Deployment of the Initial Post-War Force: Study by Assistant Chief of Air Staff Plans" (14 June 1944). 145.041A; 2–2141–60.

20. The 105-group plan, p. 6.

21. *Ibid.*   22. *Ibid.*

23. *Ibid.*, p. 4.   24. *Ibid.*, pp. 5–7.

of the post-war Air Force to the Navy, the Navy Air Arm and the Marine Corps." [25]

This ambivalence was a result of different views held within the AAF concerning the role of naval aviation. Some AAF leaders considered carriers and carrier aviation obsolescent and therefore had no interest in the AAF taking over naval aviation. It was assumed by these men that naval aviation was destined to die a painful, but inevitable, technological death due to the vulnerability of the carrier to attack and destruction by land-based strategic bombardment aircraft. That Doolittle represented this group is clear from his testimony before the Thomas Committee in November 1945:

> The carrier has reached, probably, its highest degree of development. I feel that it has reached its highest usefulness now and that it is going into obsolescence.
> The carrier has two attributes. One attribute is that it can move about; the other attribute is that it can be sunk.
> As soon as airplanes are developed with sufficient range so that they can go any place that we want them to go, or when we have bases that will permit us to go to any place that we want to go, there will be no further use for aircraft carriers. [26]

Colonel Moffat represented a second viewpoint on naval aviation. He did not envisage the demise of carrier aircraft; rather, he argued that since air was a separate medium from land and water all airplanes should belong to the Air Force, with carrier-based aircraft and aircrews trained and controlled by the postwar Air Force and lent to the Navy for carrier duty. General Norstad held a third view; he was convinced not only that carrier aviation had a role in the postwar world but that it was sufficiently differentiated from land-based aviation that the logical place for training and control was within the Navy. A fourth group, with views not very different from the third, saw naval aviation as having a separate and important role but only in the area of tactical aviation. Arnold was in this group as indicated by his testimony before the Thomas Committee.

> The flat top normally and properly does not go within range of an enemy's land-based aircraft, until after the enemy's air forces have been destroyed.
> So there is a period when strategic air power must carry the war into the enemy country to make it possible for land and sea forces to operate.
> Then we come to a phase where, with the longer range striking forces, you employ all land-based air forces—airplanes from flat tops, and everything that can come to blows with the enemy. We reach that phase because the successful operation of strategic air power has made it possible. [27]

25. *Ibid.*, pp. 13–14.
26. U.S. Senate, Committee on Military Affairs, *Hearings on S.84 and S.1482, Unification of Armed Forces*, 79th Cong., 1st sess., 1945, p. 308.
27. *Ibid.*, p. 89.

At the time this plan was drawn up there was no specific AAF policy concerning naval aviation, nor any group that asserted itself to the extent of preventing other views from being heard. Therefore, the 105-group plan incorporated the ideas of all groups and any AAF policy decision concerning naval aviation was postponed.

The IPWAF plan was pure Air Corps Tactical School doctrine, with one lesson from World War II included and others ignored. The need for escort fighters was fully incorporated into the plan with more groups of fighters (45) than of strategic bombers (42). The assumption that the Navy and Army had purely defensive roles to play in the postwar world was a reflection of the "lessons" of World War I as seen by Douhet and by U.S. AAF planners and leaders. The *blitzkrieg*, the Battle of Britain, and the German submarine campaign seemed to teach the AAF planners nothing; their faith in the effectiveness of defensive action on the ground and on the sea and of the absolute supremacy of the offensive in the air, the doctrine of the Air Corps Tactical School in the thirties, was not questioned.

The authorship of the IPWAF plan took place during a critical period in the strategic bombardment of Germany. This was a period of extremely heavy bomber losses on deep penetrations into Germany, when fighter escort could not be provided over the heavily defended target area and when flak and enemy defensive fighters were responsible for as many as 60 bombers lost on a single mission. During this time, even such enthusiastic supporters of strategic aviation as Generals Eaker and Spaatz were questioning the efficacy of unescorted long-range bombardment. Until the spring of 1943 the assumption that B-17 and B-24 aircraft in formation could defend themselves against fighters made the doctrine of the Tactical School seem valid. When the "battleplane" did not work out as a defensive weapon and the need for very-long-range escort fighters was admitted, the only substantial modification of doctrine was the incorporation of the escort fighter within the strategic mission. During the 1943–45 planning period no appreciation of the possible defensive use of guided missiles was recognized, and all comment on guided missiles reflected a belief that in the future they would contribute to the supremacy of the offensive in airpower.

The employment of anti-aircraft artillery, which had been dismissed by Douhet as "nothing other than a useless dispersion of energy and resources,"[28] was incorporated into the plan, and as a part of the AAF and not of the Army. Subsequent plans indicate that although anti-aircraft artillery was considered by the PWD to be an integral part of the Air Force defensive mission, it was not to have a very high priority. Thus, when available personnel were plentiful, a figure of 203,000 men in the AAA was proposed in enclosure D to the plan (authored by Major General Oldfield, an Army AAA officer). As an indication of the low priority of the anti-aircraft artillery mission, the plan itself states, "In

28. Giulio Douhet, *The Command of the Air*, trans. Sheila Fischer (Rome: Rivista Aeronautica, 1958), p. 46.

examining enclosure 'D' from the overall standpoint, it would appear that the size of the anti-aircraft force therein proposed is excessive in proportion to the remainder of the Air Force, if the theory is accepted that the principal defense against air attack will be found in the aggressive use of our air striking force."[29]

Although the IPWAF plan was not the only one formulated by the PWD, it was certainly the one favored of all those drawn up during the war. It indicated what the Air Corps planners desired in the postwar world in terms of force levels and correct doctrine, and it revealed which lessons they had learned from the war experience and which they had ignored. The plan received general acceptance by both AAF leadership and the rank and file who had access to it. It was not, however, accepted by the War Department, and soon after its distribution the SPD requested a new plan based on a more specific set of assumptions. As subsequent plans were drawn up, the IPWAF plan continued to be the one preferred by the PWD, and it was only in the spring of 1945 that the figure of 105 groups was reluctantly abandoned by this division.

The arbitrary nature of the 105-group figure is characteristic of all the group figures in the various AAF postwar plans. The figure was not based on any serious weighing of postwar contingencies followed by a logical analysis of how many groups might be needed to meet them. Rather, the planners selected a large figure which seemed to have some high-level War Department support and used that as the starting point in the planning process. The figure of 105 groups was accepted by the AAF planners on the suggestion of the Operations Division of the War Department. The planners envisioned that this force could police the world either through an international organization or without one. Working on the theory that in the postwar world the only other power with a strategic aviation capability would be a friendly Great Britain, the 105-group plan, heavily weighted toward strategic bombardment deployed strategically, was considered sufficient to subdue any aggressor, large or small. In the course of planning after February 1944, innumerable attempts were made by the planners to find some figure that would satisfy the basic assumptions of the 105-group plan, yet be acceptable to the Congress and the people. The 105-group, 1,000,000-man figure of the IPWAF was not a minimum force level; it was one which the planners said would provide minimum requirements for world-wide peacekeeping as well as some spare forces to meet unexpected contingencies and difficulties. The 105-group structure was the desired force throughout; the 78-, 75-, and 70-group structures which were to follow were always considered minimum force levels; and the figures of 45 groups, 65 groups, 16 groups, and 25 groups, which at various times were suggested by the War Department, were viewed by the planners as unacceptable to meet either the national defense or the international police requirements.

29. The 105-group plan, p. 10. Notice the similarity between this comment about defense against air attack and Douhet's comment on defense: ". . . how can we defend ourselves? My answer to this has always been *by attacking*." Douhet, *Command of the Air*, p. 43.

In an important memorandum to Colonel Moffat on 23 May 1944, General Kuter requested that the PWD construct an alternative plan. Anticipating budgetary difficulties with the IPWAF plan, Kuter suggested a plan based on the assumption of an effective international force for the maintenance of peace. This letter is quoted in full:

Subject: Less Expensive Post War Air Force.

1. The high annual cost of the Initial Post War Air Forces as now laid out, forces a re-study of the subject with lower cost in view.

2. Please undertake the study of a Post War Air Force of lesser size and expense, but make that force clearly contingent on some very definite and concise assumptions, one of which should be that there has been established an effective international force for the maintenance of peace.

3. I want to be sure to avoid our having a series of proposals which might be construed as bargain rate Air Forces, but feel that we must have another plan up our sleeve in the very probable event that the element of cost should become a principal consideration.[30]

Kuter apparently anticipated the contingency of an effective international organization not because he thought that it was likely to materialize but because he wanted to have ready a different set of assumptions for the smaller force in order to defend the desired IPWAF plan for the period prior to the establishment of an effective international organization.[31] In the event that such an organization were not established, the Air Force could then choose the IPWAF plan with its 105 groups and one million men. The use of an alternate set of assumptions to differentiate the IPWAF plan (105 groups) from Postwar Air Force Plan number 2 (75 groups) was a useful safeguard against anticipated War Department restrictions on force levels. In this way there was little likelihood of losing the important bargaining point that the 105-group Air Force was the only postwar Air Force which could meet the national security requirements of the United States in all postwar contingencies save the one where an international organization for the maintenance of peace was established and effective.

As in the case of the 105-group plan, the AAF planners were considerably ahead of the War Department's postwar planning. When, on 15 June 1944, the SPD requested a revised plan for an Air Force of 500,000 regulars and 200,000 trainees from the Universal Military Training program, the PWD was well on the way to devising an alternative plan.[32] No assumptions were made by the War Department concerning

30. 145.86–100; 2–2210–15.
31. Kuter never had any real faith in an international organization as a means of maintaining world peace. Kuter interview.
32. Memorandum from Brigadier General W. F. Tompkins, Director, Special Planning Division, to Commanding General AAF; Attn: Chief of Special Projects Office (15 June 1944). 145.86–76; 4434–206. The Special Planning Division received a copy of the IPWAF plan in February 1944 but was aware of its basic content by December 1943.

the postwar world situation; this left the Air Force free to make its own in conjunction with the Kuter memorandum of 23 May 1944.

Postwar Air Force plan number 2 was completed on 14 July 1944 and it incorporated the two contributions external to the PWD (the Kuter memorandum and the SPD memorandum dated 15 June) as well as ideas of the planners themselves. The assumptions made in the second part of this plan were skillfully drawn.

> PWAF Plan No. 2 . . . is based upon the following further assumptions as to the world political and military situation:
>
> a. An international organization for the maintenance of world-wide peace and security and for the regulation of armaments is in full and effective operation.
>
> e. Total power of such a world organization is adequate to insure peace against any potential aggressor, including one of the major powers.[33]

The postwar planners now had an alternative plan calling for a force structure of 75 groups and 30 separate squadrons and 685,000 men, including 200,000 trainees,[34] based on the above assumptions.

Kuter had suggested certain general assumptions for bargaining purposes; the PWD not only accepted these suggestions but modified them to incorporate highly unlikely contingencies. Kuter had suggested an assumption of an effective international peacekeeping force; the postwar planners modified this so that the organization would maintain peace and security, regulate armaments, and insure effective action against potential aggressors even if an aggressor state was a major power. In the next year there were many times when the PWD would remind the War Department that PWAF plan number 2 (75 groups) was not the AAF's primary plan and that it was only applicable when and if the assumptions made had been met.

The 75-group plan gives some insights into the planning process but it does not explain how the 70-group plan was formulated. What the 75-group plan does show is the continued opposition to budgetary and manpower restrictions and the willingness of the postwar planners to imply that they accepted the War Department guidelines without ever doing so. It should be remembered, however, that the initial War Department guideline of 105 groups was accepted by the AAF.[35]

Although the 75-group Air Force of PWAF plan number 2 was not much larger than the 70-group program, it was more than a year before the 70-group figure was established. In the interim, numerous groups and manpower figures were considered by both the War Department and the AAF. The list of suggested force structures that received some con-

---

33. "Outline of the Postwar Air Force Plan No. 2. A study prepared by AC/AS, Plans (PWD), Revised 11 August 1944." (The 11 August revision was the 15 July plan combined with the 11 August plan for anti-aircraft artillery.) 145.860–69B; 2–2141–26.

34. *Ibid.*, p. 3.

35. Above, p. 55.

sideration from the PWD is quite lengthy. During the 1943–45 period the following numbers of regular Air Force groups were either suggested by planners within the PWD or were officially received from an external source within the AAF or from the War Department or JCS: 105, 78, 75, 70, 65, 50, 45, 25, 16. Each of these figures was, in turn, varied by manipulation of numbers of squadrons per group or numbers of separate squadrons. In addition, numerous specific manpower figures were considered by the PWD; for each group figure there were usually two or more manpower figures considered. Only the highlights of these rather complex annals will be discussed.

By the summer of 1944 the AAF had produced two plans, each based on a separate set of assumptions about the postwar international environment. Neither plan made any reference to overall costs of the postwar Air Force, the War Department, or the total defense establishment. Neither did they specify how the manpower would be obtained for the sizeable regular establishment. The assumption was made by the PWD that it was the postwar planners' responsibility to determine what was required in the way of Air Force manpower and groups and up to Congress and the people to decide either how these forces were to be obtained or how these forces could be reduced to a point (which Congress must determine) that the nation could economically and politically afford.

This assumption indicated a degree of sophistication as well as a certain naïveté on the part of the postwar planners. The sophistication was evidenced when they objected to the military's imposing limitations on itself that would cause it to recommend a force structure which could not support the anticipated foreign policy aims of the United States. The argument they used was that it was the task of the military to request the forces required, on the basis of military expertise, and that it was the responsibility of other executive and congressional agencies to provide the political and economic inputs on which the decisions would be made. The naïveté was obvious in the lack of coordination with the Navy and the Army to determine what roles those services would play and what part of the overall military budget the Air Force would require to provide its portion of the national defense effort. The AAF planners, in considering the Air Force as the first line of defense, planned a force structure which was designed to defend the United States with little support from either the Army or the Navy. This is understandable in the light of the AAF doctrine of this period, as well as of the detailed AAF postwar planning which antedated similar planning by the Army or Navy. Nevertheless, to construct a number of detailed plans for the postwar world without considering the assistance that the Army and Navy might provide invited the danger of instituting an Air Force and a military establishment in excess of national needs.

Although there is evidence of nibbling by the War Department at the 685,000 manpower figure of the 75-group plan, and a tendency on the part of Army planners, specifically the SPD, to believe that the

75-group plan was the primary Air Force postwar plan, it was an event in the late fall of 1944 that dealt the first serious blow to AAF postwar planning. General Marshall rejected the G-3 Troop Basis of 19 August 1944, which called for a regular Army and Air Force of one million men, on the basis that the expense of a large regular force in addition to the expense of a program of Universal Military Training would put such a heavy burden on the economy that the combination of a large regular establishment and UMT would be unacceptable to Congress and the American people.[36]

What inspired Marshall to reject previous War Department assumptions was a November 1944 briefing by Major General George J. Richards, the War Department Budget Officer, in which Richards used the Army and Army Air Corps plans to determine the annual costs of the postwar War Department (assuming that Army and Air Force expenditures were both included in the War Department figures). Even though Richards' estimate was based on an Air Force strength approximating the PWAF plan number 2 size (75 groups), and even though his estimate for Air Force expenditures was only $3 billion, Marshall was appalled at the anticipated $7 billion cost of the combined Army and Air Force postwar structure. The estimate given to Marshall by Richards was probably the $6.8 billion estimate which the War Department Budget Office reached on 1 November 1944.[37]

On 13 November, Marshall directed the SPD to name a committee to initiate a re-survey of postwar strength using the following parameters: a balanced budget, a force maintained wholly on a volunteer basis, and Universal Military Training for all physically and mentally qualified young men. The committee made some crucial assumptions based on "many studies . . . made recently by competent economists."[38] The assumptions regarding peacetime funds available to the federal government were based on a forecast that the "annual income available to the National Treasury in normal peace years immediately after this war will not exceed 15 billion dollars (present size dollars)." This figure was divided into $6 billion for "Interest on national debts," $3 billion for "Retirement of national debts," $3 billion for "Veterans Administration," $1 billion for "Current operating costs of government other than defense," and $2 billion for "National defense."[39]

It appears that the members of this committee, realizing the mandate under which they were operating, felt obliged to reduce the $6.8 billion

36. Memorandum for General Arnold from Colonel Moffat. Subject: Report on Post-War Air Force Plans (12 December 1944), pp. 2–3. 145.86–69B; 2–2141–26.

37. Memorandum for the Advisory Council from Colonel Davison. Subject: Problems in Planning for the Postwar Air Force (13 December 1944). 1.3690–19.

38. The committee was called "The Committee for the Re-Survey of the Troop Basis for the Post-War Army." Memorandum for Record. Subject: Re-Survey of Post-War Strength, written by Colonel Moffat (25 November 1944). 145.86–57; 4334–139. It is not known who these economists were. Colonel Bonar of the War Department Budget Office formulated the assumptions.

39. *Ibid.*

figure for the annual cost of national defense which Marshall had rejected. The estimate of only $2 billion for national defense was so low that Colonel Bonar's suggestion that the $3 billion for the retirement of the national debt might be available for national defense was accepted by the committee as guidance for planning purposes, with a maximum of $5 billion being available for the Army, Navy, and Air Force, and for the Universal Military Training program. Colonel Moffat's summary of the decisions made at the second meeting of this committee showed his dissatisfaction with this figure:

> If former peacetime years can be used as a guide, this 5 billion will be divided 55% Navy, 45% Army—or $2\frac{3}{4}$ billion Navy, and $2\frac{1}{4}$ billion Army. He (Colonel Bonar) has already estimated that the cost of UMT will be $1\frac{1}{2}$ billion approximately, which will leave less than 800 million a year to the Regular Army and Air Force.[40]

The AAF planners who had computed a 105-group Air Force at a cost of $5 billion and a 75-group force at $3 billion now were faced with the problem of designing a regular Air Force based on some portion of $800 million a year. At a later meeting of this re-survey committee (27 November) the $5 billion figure for annual military and naval expenditures was retained, but the War Department share was assumed to be $2,800,000, with $1,500,000 for UMT and $200,000,000 for Reserve, National Guard, and Reserve Officer Training Corps expenses. This left $1,100,000 for the regular Army and Air Force establishment; based on a $4,000 per capita cost, a force of 275,000 was decided upon, with 120,000 for the Air Force. This would permit 16 air groups (55 squadrons) "after allowing for the personnel required for overhead and training."[41]

During November and December 1944, when the Committee to Re-Survey the Troop Basis for the Post War Army arrived at this greatly reduced personnel allocation, the AAF leaders indicated that they would not accept such an immense reduction from the AAF plans. In fact,

---

40. *Ibid.* This memorandum included background information on the Committee for the Re-Survey of the Troop Basis for the Post-War Army as well as a summary of the discussion held and the decisions taken at the second meeting of this committee on 24 November 1944. The official United States Air Force history of World War II, edited by Craven and Cate, devotes approximately three pages to the subject, "Wartime Planning for the Postwar Air Force," VII, 579–82. Unfortunately, there are a number of factual errors in this brief discussion which should be pointed out. General Kuter was not on the Committee to Re-Survey Post-War Strength (this committee is most often referred to in the AAF official files as the Committee for the Re-Survey of the Troop Basis for the Post-War Army); the meeting dates mentioned in Craven and Cate are incorrect in that the important 24 November meeting was the second meeting of this committee, while Chauncey E. Saunders, author of this portion of this history indicates that the committee did not meet between 16 and 27 November. Saunders neglects to mention the important fact that the AAF leaders and planners never accepted the "War Department Plan for the Post War Military Establishment" which was the result of the work of this committee.

41. Memorandum for the Advisory Council. Subject: Problems in Planning for the Postwar Air Force, from Colonel Davison (13 December 1944). 2–2390–19.

in December the Deputy Commander of the AAF sent a letter to all Air Forces and independent AAF commands stating that the 105-group plan would be the basis for postwar planning.[42] On 27 December the SPD sent a memorandum to General Marshall informing him of the tentative decisions made by the committee, in which were cited the figures of 120,000 men and 16 groups for the AAF.[43] On 15 January 1945 the PWD sent a memorandum to the SPD in which the AAF "non-concurred" with the 27 December report.[44] This memorandum recommended:

> a. That prior to formulation of plans for the peace-time military establishment, an estimate be prepared of the political and military situation, both internal and external, so far as it can reasonably be foreseen for the period in question.

> b. That the War Department then determine its minimum peace-time requirements for national security and draft its plans accordingly.[45]

An even more important document written by Colonel Moffat on 14 January 1945, which was rewritten and condensed to become the 15 January memorandum cited above, gives some insights into the thinking within the AAF at a time when the plans for a large postwar Air Force were being seriously challenged by General Marshall and the War Department's SPD. This document is remarkable for two reasons. First, the AAF planners had not hitherto specifically identified any possible enemies. Second, this was the first time they gave any consideration to the role of the other services in opposing these potential enemies.

> If the national defense is to be adequately provided for, it is the opinion of this Headquarters that the military authorities should first state the minimum military requirements for national security and that Congress should then determine budgetary limitations, if any. Neither past military practice nor Congressional action prior to this war is indicative of future requirements for the military establishment nor of the future temper of the people in respect to the proportionate amount of the nation's total resources which can and must be continuously devoted to the maintenance of that establishment. It is believed that the War Department should recommend to Congress and the people the minimum size Force necessary for the accomplishment of the military mission regardless of the estimates of economists based on our pre-war experience as to what they now think the nation will make available for the national security in future peacetime periods.[46]

42. Army Air Forces letter 20–8 (18 December 1944). 145.86–100; 2–2210–15.

43. Memorandum for the Chief of Staff, U.S. Army. Subject: Report of Progress on Re-Survey of the Troop Basis for the Post-War Army, from Colonel G. E. Textor (27 December 1944). 145.96–128 (111-M-B); 8090–32.

44. Memorandum for the Chief of Staff, U.S. Army. Attention: Special Planning Division. Subject: Report on Progress on Re-Survey of the Troop Basis for the Post-War Army, from Colonel R. C. Moffat (15 January 1945). 145.96–128 (111-M-B); 8090–32.

45. *Ibid.*, p. 2.

46. Memorandum for the Chief of Staff, U.S. Army (14 January 1945), p. 2.

It is asserted in paragraph 1, Tab. A. of the report (27 December report, SPD to Marshall) that because it was so in the past, approximately one-half of the future peacetime appropriation for the armed forces will go to maintenance of the Navy. That assumption is not acceptable. Prior to this war the Army Air Force was of negligible size and effectiveness as an M-day force. In the future it cannot be assumed that surface forces, even though augmented by a carrier-borne air arm, can assure security to this country against sudden and serious attack from abroad.[47]

An Air Force like a Navy requires years to create and cannot be extemporized in twelve or twenty-four months. The size of the standing Navy and Air Force must be related to those of potential enemies. After this war, it appears that only one nation in addition to the United States will emerge as a first-class Naval power, whereas both Britain and Russia will emerge as strong in Air power.[48]

All planning done within the PWD prior to this time was based on assumptions of the future world which were nonspecific in their orientation toward future adversaries and which did not take into consideration the roles of the Army and the Navy in the maintenance of national security. When threatened with extreme curtailment, the AAF planners were forced to consider budgetary constraints, the roles of the Army and the Navy, and potential enemies. The budgetary problem was handled by the rejection of the idea of self-limitation; the problem of postwar enemies was solved by identifying Russia as the one long-range postwar threat, based on its assumed airpower capability. Apparently, enemies were to be identified on the basis of what states had large air forces or might be expected to develop them.

For the first time in the AAF planning process there was a specific acknowledgment of the competition among the services for a share of the defense budget. Planning up to this time had been based on the supposition that Congress would allocate to the postwar Air Force the funds required for the 105-group or 75-group Air Force (depending on the world situation) and that what the Army and Navy would obtain was not relevant. Now, however, the planners were aware of the possibility of a budgetary ceiling on the defense establishment; and though they argued that this ceiling, if necessary at all, should be established by Congress, they also attacked the Army supposition that the monetary split among Navy, Army, and Air Force would be based on the prewar breakdown of approximately 50 per cent for the Navy and 50 per cent for the Army and AAF.

Although prior to the winter of 1944–45 there had been some awareness that in the postwar period the Navy would provide greater problems for the Air Force than would the Army, it was not until the military budget was considered in terms of percentage allotments for services that the postwar planners began to recognize that if the Air Force were

47. *Ibid.*, p. 2.
48. *Ibid.*, p. 3.

to gain in the budgetary infighting it would be at the expense of the Navy. The War Department planning called for about 25 per cent of the defense budget for the ground army, a percentage so small it did not invite appreciable reduction. The AAF planners not only resisted budgetary self-limitation, they also rejected the War Department estimate of $5 billion for the postwar defense establishment. The postwar planners anticipated a defense budget of $7.8 billion and expressed fear that most of this sum would go to the Navy.

> If the Army and the Army Air Force propose for themselves a policy of retrenchment and economy, they may find themselves standing alone in a country determined to keep the system working. The principles of disarmament are today publicly discredited. The Navy, headed by one of our most competent financiers, who is thoroughly familiar with fiscal policy, will align their objectives with those of the nation and, if the Army policy is not astute, will assume the responsibility for national defense.[49]

The postwar planners were faced with the problem of what size force structure they should recommend in view of certain budgetary limitations. Although a $5 billion figure for the entire defense budget was certainly not a firm one, there was an awareness among the planners that Congress would undoubtedly place some limitation on military expenditures which would prevent all of the services from getting all of what they wanted. Although the planners continued to advocate asking for what was required for national security, the 105-group, 1,000,000-man, $5 billion postwar Air Force began to appear unattainable.

The evolution of thinking in the spring and summer of 1945 is evident in the record. By March 1945 the 105-group program was given a terminal date of V-J Day plus three years. This had always been the program for the initial postwar period, but on the basis of the record throughout 1944 there was an implicit supposition that this 105-group figure would be necessary for the conceivable future since stringent requirements were placed on the international organization before it could be acceptable as the basis for PWAF plan number 2. The 75-group program was to start at the time the initial plan was terminated, assuming that "a working international organization" then existed. The difference between "a working international organization" required for implementation of PWAF plan number 2 as of 29 March 1945 and "an international organization for the maintenance of world-wide peace and security and for the regulation of armaments . . . in full and effective operation," in addition to the requirement that this organization be capable of ensuring peace against "any potential aggressor, including any of the major powers," required for implementation as of 11 August 1944, is obvious. As of March 1945 there was still some doubt as to the final size of the postwar Air Force, so both a 75- and a 16-group plan were drawn up.

49. Memorandum for General Norstad. Subject: Effect of Future National Fiscal Policy upon the Army Air Forces Postwar Military Establishment (29 June 1945), p. 3. 145.86–98; 2–2141–46.

By 31 May the 105-group plan had been shelved and a new force was considered the interim Air Force. This consisted of 78 groups plus 32 separate squadrons (638,286 personnel) and was to be the size of the Air Force from the end of demobilization to V-J Day plus three years. This was the third major AAF postwar plan and it replaced the 105-group plan. Although there was an occasional reference to the 105-group plan in the next several months, this was because some officers within AAF Headquarters were unaware of the impending replacement by the 78-group plan. This new plan, entitled "The Interim Air Force," was a complete replacement for the former one as it had evolved in the winter and spring of 1945.

The 78-group plan included 638,286 men and 32 separate squadrons, while the 75-group plan, which was to come into effect 3 years after V-J Day, had 485,000 men on active duty. In the formulation of the 78-group plan there was the beginning of a tendency for the sizes of the interim Air Force and of the permanent Air Force to converge. By late summer of 1945 a decision was made by General Norstad to have a single Air Force plan (for both the immediate postwar and the permanent postwar Air Force) which was the final step in the slow convergence of group and personnel levels of the two plans. During the summer of 1945 the AAF planners reduced the size of the interim Air Force but were reluctant to cut back on the permanent Air Force (since July 1944 this had been the 75-group plan). Therefore, the convergence in size of the two plans was a result of the diminishment of the interim force level to the desired level of the permanent force.

A fourth major plan, entitled the "V-J Plan," was completed on 15 July 1945. This was a lengthy demobilization proposal authored by the SPO, which marked the 78-group figure as the point at which demobilization would cease. The V-J Plan was the only significant AAF postwar plan that was not authored by the PWD; the assumptions used in its formulation were indicative of the willingness of General Davison and the staff of the SPO to base demobilization planning on parameters established by the PWD.

Where do the 70-group, 400,000-man figures, which were to become the AAF bargaining points in the 1945–50 period, come from? All the available evidence points to the fact that the 400,000-man figure is the crucial one, for the question was approached by asking into how many groups could 400,000 men be divided.[50] Since the 78 and 75 groups had

50. "Two years of planning in the Air Staff have resulted in the firm conviction that the 70 group Air Force (which has been squeezed into a 400,000 tentative Troop Basis) is the bed rock minimum with which the Air Force can accomplish its peacetime mission." Colonel Cork, "Minority Report of AAF Member of Bessell Committee" (draft) (26 October 1945). 2.145.86–50; 4334–129–6. The Bessell Committee was established by the War Department in September 1945. Its official title was Special War Department Committee on the Permanent Establishment. Memorandum to Brigadier Generals W. W. Bessell, Jr., OPD, E. W. Chamberlin, G-3, G. E. Textor, SPO, G. C. Jamison, AAF, R. E. Jenkins, AGF, Henry Wolfe, ASF, from Brigadier General H. I. Hodes, Assistant Deputy Chief of Staff. Subject: Strength of Permanent Military Establishment (15 October 1945). 145.96–128 (111-M-B); 8090–32.

been figures cited for a 638,286- and a 485,000-man establishment, respectively, a decision was made by Norstad that by "skeletonizing" force structures, 400,000 men could provide a force of 70 groups.[51] This key figure of 400,000 was the number of men the AAF planners and personnel experts anticipated could be recruited and maintained on a strictly volunteer basis.[52] All the assumptions about various contingencies and all the various plans based on alternative assumptions (though these were often manipulated) were now irrelevant. The bargaining skill of the AAF planners was manifested in their choosing two round, easy-to-grasp figures and also in their refusal to deviate by one group or one man from them. On 8 December 1945, when consideration was again being given to cutting the Air Force to 16 groups, the Air Staff, Plans, was prepared to brief Generals Arnold and Eisenhower as follows: "Therefore, after every conceivable cut [has] been effected and services pared to the bone we have stopped at the present program for 70 groups and 400,000 men. 69 or 68 *will* make a significant difference. . . ."[53] Toward the end of 1945 the planners, realizing that a 70-group figure was simple for Congress and the people to grasp, and recognizing also that 400,000 was a figure which budget cutters could more easily whittle down, talked more about "70 groups" than about 400,000 men.[54]

A further question remains. If 400,000 men was the figure the planners decided was a realistic one for an all-volunteer Air Force, did they investigate possible ways to increase voluntary enlistments to above 400,000? Throughout the war various ideas were considered which might increase the incentive for young men to volunteer for military service in peacetime. One problem that faced the planners was General Marshall's twofold restriction on the postwar War Department military establishment: he insisted that the regular establishment had to be an all-voluntary force and that self-imposed budgetary limitations could not be exceeded.

The Air Force might have expected to achieve a large voluntary force by substantially increasing the incentives that would make military service more attractive, but that would have raised the cost per individual

51. "In order to meet the 70 group, 400,000 men Air Force program it has been necessary to plan skeletonization of enlisted personnel and officers other than combat crew to 80% of total T/O in all units." Routing and Record Sheet, from AC/AS-3 to AC/AS-5, Post War Division. Subject: Strength of Permanent Military Establishment (25 October 1945). 145.86–50; 4334–129.

52. "Can the AAF maintain a force of 400,000 by voluntary enlistment? Yes, this is believed by A-1 to be possible. Even assuming fixed strength requirements for the Army and Navy it is believed the Air Force will be able to maintain a strength of 400,000 on their own." Memorandum from Garrett to Jamison (8 December 1945), p. 2.

53. *Ibid.*, p. 1.

54. Thomas C. Schelling has shown the advantage in bargaining of choosing a simple bargaining point and standing firmly on that point. *The Strategy of Conflict* (New York: Oxford University Press, 1963), p. 70. See also his discussion of commitment, in *ibid.*, chap. V.

and consequently would have increased the personnel costs of the proposed Air Force. Since the AAF knew it would be restricted by the War Department in total funds available, a cutback on research and development, operational aircraft, maintenance and training, or some other cost area would have to be made in order to counterbalance any rise in personnel costs. To avoid such self-defeating action, the AAF calculations were based on the number of men it expected it could recruit on the basis of current wartime incentives, and thus the figure of 400,000 men was settled on.

On 29 August 1945 the AAF set 70 groups as the objective for the permanent force; within the next two months this objective had become firm AAF policy for the short- and long-term postwar Air Force. Within the PWD, consideration was given to smaller force structures, but in all communications with agencies outside the AAF the figure of 70 groups was used. Thus, the 70-group Air Force—which was to have such an important impact on the interservice competition, the UMT versus no UMT contest, and the congressional and executive wrangle over the military budget in the period between World War II and the Korean conflict—was set after a two-year period of evolution. By the summer of 1945 the planners were aware that presenting two plans and two force structures to the War Department was unwise, due to the tendency of that department to ignore the larger force structure. Also, since a series of cutbacks had not appeased the SPD, the AAF leaders feared that unless a specific force structure was presented, the nibbling away would continue until the Air Force was reduced to 16 groups.

The 70-group figure was also based on the mobilization requirement of being able to expand to an Air Force of 1,500,000 men one year after M-Day, the perceived need to keep aircraft production at such a level that mobilization requirements could be met in terms of materiel production, the need to man with regular forces "the essential bases for protection of the country's interest," and the need to have a "Mobile Striking Force" of 25 very-heavy bomb-groups.[55] Using a base planning figure of 5,000 men for each tactical group, 350,000 men would be needed to man the 70 groups. There remained 50,000 men to carry out certain training responsibilities outside the scope of the regular establishment.

The 70-group program was the culmination of a great deal of planning within the PWD, together with numerous external inputs which affected the size level but not the basic doctrine or suppositions under which the planners operated. The 70-group program was basically the 105-group structure cut down to a bare minimum. The detailed planning done for the 105-group program was absent in the 70-group program, but there can be little doubt that the basic suppositions remained the same. The United States would maintain postwar peace either through an international organization or through unilateral action by means of

55. Memorandum for General Jamison, signed by L/Col. K. L. Garrett (8 December 1945), p. 2.

airpower, which not only must be the strongest military force in the world but must have the kind of absolute superiority that would prevent one or more states from seriously challenging United States policy.[56]   For such a tall order, 70 groups seemed a minimum, irreducible force level.

56. "*THE THIRD PERIOD—Beginning with the successful establishment of an effective functioning World Security Organization and continuing into the unforeseeable future.*

"*Mission of the Air Force in the Third Period.*

"f. To maintain in being a total air strength greater than that any single nation or likely combination of nations can dispose, as an indispensable background for diplomatic negotiations."   Plans for the Post-War Air Force: Outline for General Norstad (4th Draft, 1 May 1945), pp. 2–4.   145.86–100; 2–2210–15.

6

The Selection of Air Bases

A fundamental task facing the planners was the selection of air bases for the postwar world which would meet the operational and training needs of a large and diversified Air Force. The rationale behind their selection of numbers and locations of air bases gives some interesting insights into the motivational considerations underlying the choice of bases as well as into the strategic preconceptions of the planners.

Although the identification of the short-term enemy, Japan, and the long-term enemy, Russia, had a direct effect on the planning for bases, the principal concern of the postwar planners was their need to justify a large postwar air force. The AAF's desire to obtain overseas bases had a direct relationship to its wish for a large portion of the defense budget. If a requirement for many overseas bases could be justified, then half the battle for funds would be won. Bases, to be useful offensive and defensive strongholds, required both types of aircraft; the more overseas bases that could be justified, the greater was the likelihood that approval of a large number of groups could be obtained. This, in turn, would permit an Air Force of sufficient size to require continual replacement of aircraft, the ongoing operation of the aircraft industry, and the uninterrupted development of new weapons systems. Justification for overseas bases was therefore an important step in the AAF planners' attempt to justify a 105-group and later a 70-group Air Force. Each overseas base was to be manned with one bomber and one fighter group with the argument that bases must serve to defend the United States in two ways: with all possible air routes to this country protected through the overseas basing of defensive fighters and by deterrence with bases close enough to all potential enemies so that bombers could reach targets within the strategic heartland of any potential adversary.

In July 1943, General Handy tentatively divided the 105 groups into geographical areas as follows: 30 in the European Theater, 25 in the Pacific Theater, and 50 in the continental United States and its possessions. Although the authors of the IPWAF plan used Handy's 105-group figure, they deviated appreciably from his geographical deployment. The IPWAF deployment schedule for planning purposes was as follows:

e. That one Air Force will be deployed in the Atlantic-European-African area comprised of 10VHB, 10F and 1TC groups [21 groups].

f. That two Air Forces will be deployed in the Pacific-Asiatic area aggregating 25VHB, 1HB, 25F, 1 Recon and 6TC groups [58 groups].

g. That three Air Forces will be deployed in the U.S. (including Alaska and the Caribbean) aggregating 5 VHB, 1HB, 4M/LB, 10F, 2 Recon and 4TC groups [26 groups].[1]

There is a noticeable shift from Handy's plan, in which the main air force strength was located in the continental United States, to the IPWAF plan with its emphasis on strength in the Pacific and Far East. Handy envisioned a force of 25 groups in the Pacific, while Hamilton, Moffat, and the PWD anticipated a need for 58 groups (more than 55 percent of the postwar Air Force strength) in that area.

Here, for the first time in the postwar planning process, was an indication of "Mercator projection" thinking in the PWD, which remained evident throughout the rest of the planning period despite occasional mention of threats from the direction of the poles, great-circle routes, and polar projections. A December 1942 map showed the air defense vulnerabilities as perceived by AAF planners for the period of the war. The map showed areas along the eastern and western coastlines of the United States, with no areas to the north illustrated except for one covering most of Lake Superior and parts of Lakes Michigan and Huron.[2] Although this was not an unrealistic estimate in 1942, there is no evidence that in the 1944–45 period the planners grasped the strategic significance of the northern approaches to the United States. General Handy, the Assistant Chief of Staff of the Army, a ground officer with no Air Corps background, had a more sophisticated grasp of strategic bombardment, long-range aircraft navigation, great-circle routes, and so forth, than did the AAF men doing the planning. A 30 May 1945 status report, authored by Lieutenant Colonel P. Shepley of the PWD, stated: "Within the Continental U.S. combat units will be stationed on selected airbases along the East and West Coasts for defensive purposes, while the intervening central areas will accommodate training and administrative activities."[3]

An indication of the curious thinking concerning very-long-range aircraft traversing a world that was spherical rather than flat was indicated in Hamilton's reply to Davison's query about diversification of aircraft and allied industries.

> 2. A secondary factor will be to guard against concentration along either seaboard or too close to the northern or southern boundaries of Continental United States.

As has been stressed in Air Force recommendations for the postwar military requirement of air bases, the range of postwar bombardment aircraft will presumably be so great that attack along great circle routes across polar regions must be considered as likely as attack from either sea frontier.[4]

1. The 105-group plan, pp. 6–7. In this period very heavy bombers were B-29's; heavy bombers, B-17's and B-24's; medium bombers, B-25's.
2. 145.81–81; 3640–9.
3. 145.86–2; 4334–59.
4. Memorandum to Special Projects (Colonel Davison) from AC/AS Plans (written by Hamilton, signed by Kuter) (2 October 1943).

The danger from the direction of the poles was perceived, yet no differentiation in relative danger between northern and southern approaches to the United States was made.

With respect to stationing aircraft in the closest proximity to possible postwar threats, again there was some indication that the planners envisioned the world in Mercator terms. Not one polar projection appeared among the many maps used by the PWD to illustrate deployment of forces. As late as October 1945, Arnold, though showing some grasp of the necessity of using maps that more accurately portrayed great-circle routes, showed no appreciation of the relative strategic differences between polar routes to the north and those to the south.

> I have here a chart. Most of you who were down in my office saw the new type of chart that we use in considering future air operations.
>
> Instead of using the normal Mercator projection, we use a polar because, with the airplane as we now employ it, we are not limited in air operations, as in the past, by the ice and blizzards of the Arctic regions, or by the bad weather in the Tropics.[5]

Whenever ranges of various aircraft were illustrated, a simple circle of combat radius was drawn around every proposed base, with no consideration that these circles should have varied with latitude on a Mercator projection. The lack of sophistication in conceiving avenues of approach to the United States, or routes of attack by bombardment aircraft of the United States, may partially explain why little consideration was given to acquiring base rights in Canada and planning for bases in the northern sections of the United States for purposes of air defense and offensive strategic bombardment.

The IPWAF plan was supplemented by a 14 June 1944 study on the deployment of the IPWAF for Period III. (Period III was defined as the period commencing with "the ratification by the nations concerned of an international agreement designed to ensure a stabilized world peace of indefinite duration.")[6] Lacking specific guidance as to assumptions for this period the AAF planners provided their own.

> In the absence of any premise of that nature [world situation during this period] approved for planning purposes either by the Joint Chiefs of Staff . . . or by the War Department, a military situation as described below is assumed to exist at the beginning of the post-war period:
>
> a. The United States is at peace with all other nations and, discounting minor disturbances, a state of peace prevails throughout the world.
>
> b. An international world peace conference has been held and peace settlements have been ratified by all nations concerned.

5. Arnold's testimony before the Thomas Committee (19 October 1945), U.S. Senate, Committee on Military Affairs, *Hearings on S.84 and S.1482, Unification of Armed Forces*, 79th Cong., 1st sess., 1945, p. 74.
6. Deployment of the Initial Post-War Air Force: Study by Assistant Chief of Air Staff, Plans (14 June 1944). 145.041A–20; 2–2141–60.

c. The former Axis partners have been totally disarmed. Great Britain, the Union of Soviet Socialist Republics and, to a lesser extent, the Republic of China are the only military powers besides the United States capable of immediately waging war on a large scale.

d. France is re-arming, but on a limited scale due to the war-stricken economy of that nation.

e. The United States has assumed international obligations jointly with the other great powers to perform its part under the machinery established for maintenance of world peace. While Great Britain and Russia have undertaken to enforce peace in Europe and in most of Asia, the United States has accepted responsibility for enforcing peace in the Pacific and in particular for enforcing—with the assistance of China—Japan's compliance with her treaty obligations.

f. Korea and Manchuria have been freed from Japanese control. The former Japanese mandated islands have been brought under United States' sovereignty. The Philippine Islands have been granted independence but allow military base facilities to the United States.[7]

This plan differed somewhat from the 105-group plan. Although it called for a greater number of the 105 groups deployed overseas (91), approximately half of this 91 "will normally be maintained at stations within the continental United States"[8] (basically a return to Handy's tentative deployment schedule).

Another interesting point was made in the discussion portion of this study which was not evident in the 105-group plan:

10. History and reason indicate that it is only from Europe and Asia that a serious attack against the Western Hemisphere can be launched and that the northern latitudes provide the shortest routes of approach to the vital military areas in the Western Hemisphere.[9]

This discussion was used to justify the deployment of groups to Shemya and Amchitka Islands in the Aleutians, Elmendorf and Ladd Fields in Alaska, Harmon and Argentia Fields in Newfoundland, and Meeks and Patterson Fields in Iceland (Dow Field at Bangor, Maine, was considered an overseas deployment base in this study).[10] The total number of groups assigned to defend the northern areas was fourteen—seven very-heavy-bomb groups and seven fighter groups. However, since half of all overseas forces were to be held in reserve within the U.S., only seven groups were to be permanently on station at these northern bases to defend the northern approaches to the United States. The deployment of forces did not correspond with the discussion quoted above

7. *Ibid.*, pp. 3–4.
8. "In order to take advantage of the potential mobility of tactical air units, provide a strategic reserve, and to facilitate training, maintenance, and supply...." *Ibid.*, p. 6.
9. *Ibid.*, p. 5.
10. *Ibid.*, Tab "A," pp. 1–2.

concerning the vulnerability from the north, for the great preponderance of the overseas forces were deployed in the Western and Central Pacific and the Caribbean. In the process of coordination within the Air Staff, Plans, some of the implicit assumptions upon which this deployment schedule was based were seriously questioned, yet no appreciable changes seem to have been made in the final form of the study.

On 26 May 1944, Colonel R. C. Lindsay, Chief of the Combined and Joint Staff Division of the Air Staff, Plans, stated:

> 4. Military Situation: The subject paper assumes an allied victory and world peace, total disarmament of our present enemies, and emergence of the U.S., Great Britain, Russia and, to a lesser extent China, as the only major military powers in the world. This study then deploys our air force to defend the U.S., its territories and interests in general, and to enforce the peace terms, imposed upon our late enemies. Deployment as outlined in this paper points, then—within our sphere of influence in the Pacific—at a foe rendered, by our own assumption, impotent. Only our erstwhile allies are capable of major military effort and it should be pointed out that realistic planning must provide for protection against the real threat. Such considerations might well indicate a much greater concentration of force in Alaska and the Aleutians.[11]

The thinking in the PWD seemed to be that the greatest immediate threat to the United States rested with a resurgent Japan and that therefore the United States should place large air contingents within close striking distance of the Japanese islands. The apparent lack of concern with a similarly resurgent Germany seemed to be based on the theory, already mentioned, that Great Britain and Russia could take care of that problem and that a balance of power would establish itself within Europe which would free the United States from any threat from that area. The planners apparently felt that the combination of British air, sea, and land power would offset the Russian military strength, while the combination of Britain and Russia in Europe would contain postwar Germany. Colonel Lindsay (who seriously questioned the assumption that Japan would present the primary threat), being on the periphery of the postwar planning process, was able to express his doubts but could not make an appreciable impression upon the planners or their plans.

At about the same time that the deployment plan of the IPWAF was being circulated within the AAF staff sections, another study by the PWD was prepared, "To determine the AAF's post-war interests in the islands of the South and East Pacific, and to recommend action by the AAF in accordance therewith."[12] The assumptions included here illustrate lucidly the kind of strategic thinking that prevailed within the PWD during this period.

11. Memorandum to Kuter from Lindsay (26 May 1944), p. 2. 145.041A-20; 2–2141–60.

12. Memorandum (no title) for Colonel Moffat from Colonel Harry C. Wisehart (30 June 1944), p. 1. 145.86–67; 4334–161–5.

It is assumed:

(2) That the United States will be expected or delegated by the world-wide security organization to maintain a state of peace in the Pacific Ocean.

(4) That the most probable route of aggression against the Western Hemisphere by any future Asiatic power lies over those Pacific islands contained between the latitudes 30 degrees North and 30 degrees South.[13]

Assumption number four illustrates two important facets of the conceptual framework of AAF planning. The assumption was made that the next war would be initiated as the last one was, and that an extrapolation of the United States most recent historical experience with war to its next experience was valid. The assumption was made by the planners that the most likely approaches for armed attack were latitudinal rather than longitudinal. The mention in the deployment study of great-circle approaches (although certainly of small consideration in the prescriptive portions of that plan) was not even included in this study; on the contrary, "Mercator projection" thinking seems to have been unquestioned.

Three possible conditions were envisioned in the Pacific Ocean area: (1) no possibility that an Asiatic nation would become an aggressive world power; (2) any world power in Asia or Eurasia would be friendly to the United States; or, (3) an Asiatic or Eurasian nation would become a world power with a secret plan for aggression in the Pacific or even against the Western Hemisphere.[14] Working with the third contingency after quickly disposing of the first two as unrealistic, the authors of this study indicated their perception of the ". . . most important problem. No one can deny that, sometime in the future—maybe 20 years—maybe 100 years—it is possible for an Eurasian nation to grow into an aggressive-minded power."[15]

The route of attack presumed by the planners was the East Indies, followed by a steady advance toward the east using the many "stepping stones" provided by the islands between latitudes 30 degrees North and 30 degrees South. To prevent such a course of action by a possible future enemy, maintenance of a strong presence in the Central and Western Pacific was recommended.

The use of the terms "Asiatic" and "Eurasian" (nations) is indicative of what nation the postwar planners anticipated would be the potential threat to American national security. The evolution in the uses of these two terms began when the danger of any Asiatic nation was contemplated; in the next sentence the danger of a future world power in Asia or Eurasia is hypothesized; within a few paragraphs a Eurasian nation is considered the most dangerous possibility.[16] This semantic evolution, combined with the comment, "History has taught us that:

13. *Ibid.,* pp. 1–2.　　14. *Ibid.,* p. 3.
15. *Ibid.,* pp. 4–5.　　16. *Ibid.,* pp. 3–4.

80

our Allies of today may be leagued against us tomorrow," [17] makes an un-subtle reference to the danger the Soviet Union would present in the Far East in the long-term postwar period. The Soviet Union alone met the criteria of being a Eurasian nation and a wartime ally of the United States.

The IPWAF plan, the deployment study, and the study to deter-mine the AAF interests in the islands of the South and East Pacific, all prepared by the PWD in the first six months of 1944, illustrate an immediate postwar concern with a resurgent Japan. AAF policy in September 1944 concerning use of Aleutian and Alaskan bases was that these bases would be primarily for defense against a resurgent Japan and, until the signing of a peace treaty with that country, would be held on a standby basis. [18] The long-term concern was with Russia, and there was practically no concern about a resurgent Germany.

Having pointed out to all but the most naïve that the Soviet Union was the most likely long-term potential enemy in the Far East, it is difficult to explain why this assumption was followed by the assumption that the danger rested geographically between latitudes 30 North and 30 South. The state of technological development, with the United States and Great Britain the only two states which by 1944 had developed long-range operational bomber aircraft, may have been one reason why the danger from across the North Pole did not seem an important con-sideration to the postwar planners.

The need for fighter escort was another limitation on long-range bombardment. With the B-29 operational by 1944, and the B-35 and B-36 expected to be in the air by 1946, the range of the bomber was rapidly outdistancing that of the fighter; this restricted range of escort fighters was, by 1944, the gravest limitation to the strategic bom-bardment mission. Thus, long-range bombing missions directed against the United States by an enemy at such distances that fighter escort was impossible probably appeared suicidal to the planners, and therefore as an unlikely contingency—at least until the enemy had captured bases which were within fighter range of the United States.

As for the development of very-long-range bombardment aircraft by potential enemies, there was clear indication that General Arnold and the postwar planners had little respect for the technological abilities of the Soviet Union. Alexander de Seversky, the aviation engineer and aircraft manufacturer, recalls meeting Arnold at Orly airport near Paris when Arnold was en route to the Potsdam Conference and mention-ing to him the danger the Soviet Union might present in the postwar world. Arnold replied that he perceived no danger because of the primitive nature of Soviet technology. [19] This deprecation of Soviet

17. *Ibid.*, p. 4.
18. Letter to Commanding General, Eleventh Air Force, Anchorage, Alaska. Subject: Postwar Disposition of AAF Housing and Equipment, from Brigadier General P. W. Timberlake, Deputy Chief of Air Staff (25 September 1944). 145.96–125 (111-M); 8091–85.
19. Interview with Alexander de Seversky, 30 March 1966.

technology led the planners into thinking that if the Soviets were the threat in the future they would not be a threat for at least twenty years, mainly because without technological sophistication they would be unable to threaten the continental United States. How could the Soviets attack the U.S. without a large, efficient Air Force and Navy to go along with the mass armies which had stopped Hitler? Russia was strong in defense when she had the great incentive of fighting for the very soil of Mother Russia, with the advantage of short lines of communication, with the great land masses in the rear to allow retreat without defeat, with the unequal advantage of the Russian winter, which in the last three centuries had worked in her favor. But would Russia be an offensive threat? As the AAF planners judged the situation, only in the distant future could Russia become a serious threat to the national security of the United States.

There was definitely some latent imperialism in the overseas base requirements formulated by the postwar planners. This was particularly evident in their desire to secure bases in Latin America.

> The attitude of the Latin and South American countries with respect to any expansion program on the part of the United States must at all times be favorable so as to be able to gain the points needed in the answering of a problem so gigantic as this one without being offensive, or to insure the least degree of offensiveness on the part of this country. Nevertheless, this problem is a great one. Though it be distasteful to a small Latin or South American country to allow the United States to maintain and operate sufficient bases on the soil over which they have sovereignty, with reluctance, we must go ahead and plan, construct and occupy these necessary areas.[20]

The unknown author of this draft may not have been able to incorporate his ideas into AAF policy (there is no evidence that he did), but his justification of preclusive imperialism indicates the means which some of the AAF planners were willing to use to gain their ends.

These Latin American bases had little strategic value in the impending age of the very-long-range bomber, yet to at least one AAF planner they were valuable enough for him to recommend curtailment of Franklin Roosevelt's good-neighbor policy and to justify armed attack and colonization of parts of Latin American states. Although "Mercator projection" thinking is not evident in this desire for bases in Latin America, that the planners wanted these bases is indicative of their inability to grasp the

20. Draft paper. Subject: United States Interests in South America (undated and unsigned). 148.33; 4334–82–19. The grammar in the last portion of this quoted material was of such quality that I decided to modify it for purposes of clarity. The original text follows: "Nevertheless, this problem is a great one and should it be distasteful to a small Latin or South American country to allow the United States to maintain and operate sufficient bases in their general area or on the soil over which they hold sovereignty in order to protect them from future aggressive nations as well as to insure the national security of the United States itself even tho [sic] with reluctance we must go ahead and plan, construct and occupy these necessary areas."

strategic significance of the combination of a spherical planet, the location in the Northern Hemisphere of all the major powers, and the long, but not unlimited, range of strategic bombardment aircraft.

There is strong evidence that the planners seriously believed in the strategic value of these bases as a defense against bombardment of the United States from the south (by major powers that might acquire bases in South America) as well as for defense of the Panama Canal. The importance of the bases was more than *just* strategic, however. Also relevant was their use in the justification of a large Air Force. A strategic base had to be manned to be effective, and, using the logical criteria of a bombardment and a fighter group for each base, the greater the number of overseas bases, the larger would be the group requirement for the postwar force. A useful illustration of bases justifying force levels is a draft of a "Five minute talk on the plan for the Interim Air Force," written by Colonel Cork of the PWD. "The Caribbean force is considered the minimum to take care of the areas and bases involved." [21]

The selection of bases within the United States was not founded on strategic considerations either. Factors such as length of runway, landing approaches, weather conditions, taxi and parking facilities, and morale factors were the primary considerations. [22] There seemed to be a supposition that improved strategic bombardment aircraft would have such a great range capability that location of bases within the United States determined by strategic considerations would no longer be applicable. This reasoning is difficult to understand in light of the planners' assumption that the range of the B-36 was 10,000 miles—hardly an unlimited distance on a planet with a circumference of 25,000 miles—especially when this meant a combat radius of only 5,000 miles. Apparently, the great increase in range that the B-36 was expected to provide (the 1,600 mile combat radius of the B-29 was the greatest available in the 1943–45 period) and the label of "intercontinental bomber" given to this new aircraft caused the planners to neglect its range limitations. This planning was done prior to the consideration of one-way missions, which developed in the late 1940's. Also, air refueling was not a consideration, since wartime tests had been less than satisfactory and the planners considered a 10,000 mile range sufficient to handle any strategic need.

21. (7 June 1945), p. 3. 145.86–52; 4334–131.
22. Memorandum for Chief of Air Staff. Subject: Development of Air Fields for B-36 Air Bases, from Brigadier General Robert Kauch, Chief, Air Installations Division (5 April 1945). 145.86–33B; 4334–147. Also memorandum for Brigadier General P. W. Timberlake (same subject) from Moffat (6 April 1945). 145.86–33B; 4334–147.

7

Marshall, the Budget, and UMT

Planning for postwar contingencies involved more than just making assumptions about the postwar world, identifying potential enemies and possible routes of attack, evaluating the role that an international organization might play in maintaining peace, and determining required domestic and overseas bases. The questions of force levels, ratio between regular and reserve forces, mobilization schedules, and training requirements had to be faced by both War Department and Army Air Force planners. Without the manpower to meet various contingencies, policy could not be implemented. Around the force-level question revolved the question of Universal Military Training, and around the question of UMT revolved that of the professional army versus the citizen army.

The debate over UMT, which not only held the interest of Congress and the American people from 1945 to 1948 but also played an important role in the discussion about military budgets in the immediate postwar period, began during the 1943–45 period within the War Department. The policy positions reached by the AAF and the Army before the end of the war help to explain why the public debate of 1945 and 1946, which was basically one of UMT versus no UMT, had evolved by 1947 into a UMT versus a 70-group Air Force debate. The demise of the Universal Military Training Program, despite the wholehearted support of that program by Marshall and Truman, can largely be explained by the alternative the AAF provided Congress—a 70-group Air Force which would require a reasonably small number of men, 400,000, and would provide a powerful military deterrent force.[1]

The cordial relationship between Marshall and Arnold and the almost universal respect for Marshall among the Air Force leaders and planners tended to obscure the fundamentally antithetical positions of the AAF leadership and Marshall on the organization and composition of military forces in peacetime. Marshall was basically Jeffersonian in outlook, while Arnold, Kuter, and the planners were basically Hamiltonian.[2] The debate that had taken place within and without the United

1. "Congress added $822 million to Air Force appropriations, and the UMT legislation died in Committee." Samuel P. Huntington, *The Common Defense: Strategic Programs in National Politics* (New York: Columbia University Press, 1961), p. 372. Millis has pointed out that UMT might have had some application in 1914 but was outmoded by 1945. *Arms and Men: A Study in American Military History* (New York: G. P. Putnam, 1956), p. 308.

2. For a useful discussion of various American thoughts about American military policy, see Russell F. Weigley, *Towards an American Army: Military Thought from Washington to Marshall* (New York: Columbia University Press, 1962), esp. chap. XIII, "John McAuley Palmer and George C. Marshall: Universal Military Training."

States military for more than a century and a half continued in the 1943–45 period; the focus of the debate was the issue of UMT, with Marshall and his fellow Jeffersonians firmly committed to its implementation in the postwar world, and with the Air Force leaders moving from a 1943 position of support to a 1945 position of non-support.

Marshall, the lifelong professional soldier of uncommon dedication to the defense of his country, was fundamentally opposed to a large professional military force because of his belief that such a force was a danger to the democratic values of the United States. During the war, he made these points:

> There has long been an effort to outlaw war for exactly the same rea-
> son that man has outlawed murder. But the law prohibiting murder does
> not of itself prevent murder. It must be enforced. The enforcing power,
> however, must be maintained on a strictly democratic basis. There must
> not be a large standing army subject to the behest of a group of schemers.
> The citizen-soldier is the guarantee against such a misuse of power.[3]

He was also convinced that the nation would not support a large, peace-time professional force. Marshall's solution to the problem of providing adequate forces for the defense of the United States while avoiding the dangers of a large regular force was a system of universal military training which would insure a large pool of civilians with military training who could be rapidly mobilized in time of need.

The AAF position throughout the entire planning period was that a large regular Air Force was necessary to provide the deterrent and, if necessary, the offensive force to discourage or defeat any potential aggressor. This position was similar to that of Emory Upton, Elihu Root, and Peyton March; but it was Douhet's ideas, adapted to the problem of American security, that were the foundation for the Air Force position.[4] The AAF planners were firmly committed to the Douhetan doctrine of the ascendancy of the offensive in military aviation; without a large strategic bombardment force, fully trained and ready to take quick action, the planners could not guarantee the United States national security. The possible internal danger to democracies of large professional military forces was either considered irrelevant or of such lesser danger than external threats to the United States that it could be ignored in the planning process. The UMT debate between the Army and the AAF leaders was one-sided in that the AAF never faced this issue.

As early as August 1943, AAF planners were seriously questioning the value of a system of UMT to the postwar Air Force. The initial objections were based on the time required to train air-crew personnel,

3. *The War Reports of General of the Army George C. Marshall, General of the Army H. H. Arnold, Fleet Admiral Ernest J. King* (New York: Lippincott, 1947), p. 290.
4. For a discussion of the ideas of Upton, Root, March, and others concerning the professional military forces, see Weigley, *Towards an American Army*.

based on the experience of the war; that is, a universal training system based on a year's training would not allow sufficient time. Such training was then taking twenty months, and it was anticipated that technological developments in the postwar world would make training even more difficult, with a period of twenty-four months a possible postwar requirement.[5] AAF efforts to get the trainee time under the UMT program extended beyond the one-year period were unsuccessful, due to the War Department's anticipation of congressional rejection of a period in excess of a year.[6] The problem of having a balanced, trained force based on the UMT program plagued the planners throughout the war, since air crews and maintenance specialists could not be prepared in a year; and without trained air crews and maintenance men a postwar standby air force could hardly be effective upon mobilization.[7]

Colonel Moffat, who seemed unable to grasp the deficiencies in the UMT program, was generally a supporter of it for the postwar Air Force, while Colonel Davison, head of SPO, had serious reservations about a system that provided a training period of only a year and would require such a large training cadre of regular Air Force personnel. Within the PWD a number of officers questioned UMT but were not able to convince Moffat that the disadvantages outweighed the advantages as far as the Air Force was concerned. A July 1944 study by one of Moffat's staff officers, which weighed the pros and cons of UMT, is a good indication of AAF thinking about it and about how useful it might be to the Air Force.

3. g. Universal Military Training will eventually bring about some military education of our political leaders who through a better understanding of military problems will more readily vote necessary funds for military purposes.

3. j. Universal Military Training might create in the American people a frame of mind that would induce us to strike first to prevent or shorten the next war when the element of surprise may be all-important. Our time-honored custom of giving the enemy every advantage and allowing him to strike first might prove fatal in the face of deadlier weapons and methods of warfare of the future.[8]

5. Memorandum to Colonel P. M. Hamilton from Colonel F. G. Allen (21 August 1943). 141.041A; 2–2141–69.

6. "From the standpoint of practical politics, Colonel Textor advised that a training period longer than one year would never get by Congress (in UMT law)." Colonel Textor was Assistant Director (to General Tompkins) of the Special Planning Division, WDSS (War Department Special Staff). DAR, AC/AS-5, 9 November 1944.

7. By November 1944, the AAF planners were trying to devise alternatives to UMT for the training of air crews for the inactive force: "Preliminary examination indicates this to be the critical personnel problem governing rapid conversion of the peacetime air force to war strength, during the first 18 months of emergency." DAR, AC/AS-5, 27 November 1944.

8. "Universal Military Training, a Study by Assistant Chief of Air Staff, Plans" (draft). 145.86–84; 4334–208. Author unknown.

Although the author concluded that the advantages outweighed the disadvantages and that UMT would be of value to the postwar Air Force, his discussion of the disadvantages left some doubt as to where his preference lay.

4. a. Universal Military Training does not insure adequate defense. It is no substitute for a strong permanent establishment.

b. Universal Military Training may weaken the permanent establishment by turning it into a training organization as distinguished from a strategic and tactical force.

f. Socialogy [*sic*] should not be confused with defense. Health, education, crime prevention etc. are not the concern of the armed services.[9]

Moffat, dissatisfied with the strong counterarguments and the weak case for UMT, criticized the author for "a lack of conviction that it is *necessary*. That the very life of the nation may, and probably will, depend on it."[10] Davison pointed out the disadvantages of UMT to Moffat, on a number of occasions. However, since Davison considered the Air Force decision one that the Air Staff, Plans, must make, he was willing to accept the Moffat decision that it was an essential element in the postwar Air Force.[11]

General Kuter generally supported UMT on the grounds that it was needed within the Army and that it would not harm the postwar Air Force. However, when Kuter recognized that it might be a threat to a large permanent postwar Air Force, he changed his position from a lukewarm acceptance of the program (a position he held from 1943 until the autumn of 1944) to a position that it might destroy the capability to fight when hostilities began. If given a choice between a large regular force and a small regular force combined with a system of UMT, Kuter was firmly behind the abandonment of UMT.[12] The tentative decision within the

9. *Ibid.*, p. 3.

10. *Ibid.*, p. 4. Colonel Moffat's comments were written by hand at the bottom of page 4.

11. Letter from Davison to the Air Staff, Plans. Subject: Universal Military Training (1 July 1944). 145.86–84; 4334–208. In this letter, Davison expressed his objections to UMT.

". . . certain influential individuals have challenged the feasibility of any plan for universal service on these grounds:

a. The contemplated peacetime protection force of the U.S. will probably be comprised of sizeable air and naval forces with a relatively small standing Army.

b. The Air and Naval forces require so much skilled personnel that any program of one year of compulsory service for all men will not provide a period of sufficient duration to train or man adquately [*sic*] any reasonable portion of the Air or Naval forces.

c. Because of the above, universal service would be of no real help to the country when so few can be adequately trained or utilized in the AAF or Naval service.

2. These assertions are true in part, and if Universal training is to be assumed in further planning cogent reasons are required as to how applicable such a program will be to the Air Force needs."

12. Memorandum for General Arnold from General Kuter (17 January 1945). 145.86–29; 4334–204–9.

War Department to reduce the peacetime Army and Air Force to a total of 275,000 officers and men (five Army divisions and sixteen Air Force tactical groups) alerted Kuter to the heavy reliance placed upon UMT as a deterrent to aggression—a reliance he had never accepted. He was willing to accept UMT as an adjunct to, but not as a substitute for, a large regular Air Force.

It was not until March 1945, when Arnold specifically questioned UMT, that the AAF officially informed the War Department that it could not accept such a system as a replacement for large forces-in-being.[13] The reluctance of the AAF leaders to present their objections to the War Department (despite early qualms about the efficacy of such a system for the Air Force) may be explained, in part, by the great enthusiasm shown by General Marshall for it. Marshall, considered by AAF leaders and planners a great ally in the struggle for autonomy, was not to be questioned on UMT until it appeared that it was a threat to the postwar Air Force regular establishment. Davison was ready to question UMT in early 1944, Kuter by late 1944, Arnold only in March 1945. By March 1945, however, the AAF position was clear: UMT should be rejected, if its cancellation would mean a larger regular establishment.

The arguments used by Arnold in this important March 1945 memorandum to Marshall are indicative of the thinking within the Air Staff, Plans, when the plans for 105 and 75 groups were threatened by a War Department plan that allowed the Air Force only 16 groups. Almost two years of planning preceded this memorandum, and the author, Colonel Philip Cole of the PWD, had many arguments to call upon as he prepared the Arnold communication to Marshall.

The most cogent argument was that planning for a postwar military structure,

... on any basis other than that of determination of minimum requirements for national security is deemed unsound.

... it is strongly urged that there be prepared and considered an alternate plan for the peacetime military establishment, based on an analysis of military requirements. ...[14]

The UMT issue illustrated that the Air Force planners were unwilling to accept budget limitations imposed by the War Department if they precluded a large regular Air Force. Unlike many military men, the planners did not attempt to be economists or to anticipate what "the economy can stand." Many military leaders in the 1943–45 period, though very hesitant to make political calculations, showed no restraint

13. Memorandum for Marshall from Arnold (30 March 1945). 145.96–128 (111-M-B); 8090–32. This memorandum was written by Colonel Cole of the Post War Division.

14. *Ibid.*, pp. 1, 4.

in making economic calculations. Marshall was certainly the most obvious amateur economist in the military at the time.

> I don't think you could raise a large standing Army in time of peace, nor do I think you could possibly afford it, unless you go far deeper into our financial resources than the American people would permit. That leaves us with just one course for the rapid creation of a trained dependable organization, universal military training.[15]

Whenever the War Department imposed a budgetary ceiling or a manpower or group ceiling based on a budgetary restriction, the AAF planners would always protest that budgetary self-limitation was not the task of the military. In their view, the military's responsibility was to point out how much was needed for national defense while Congress held the main responsibility for determining whether or not economic factors would require some reduction of these estimates. The War Department case for UMT was based on a number of factors:

1. It was more democratic than either selective service or a large standing Army.
2. It would allow a reduced defense budget since it would drastically reduce expensive regular forces.
3. A large volunteer military was not a postwar possibility and UMT plus a small volunteer military was better than a large regular military which must be obtained, in part, by selective service.
4. UMT provided good physical, mental, and moral training for youth.[16]

The Air Force indicated that all these arguments were irrelevant so far as the military was concerned. According to the planners the important question was what military structure could best provide for the national defense. Their answer to that question was based on their assumptions of the postwar political, economic, and technological environment: first priority to on-hand, regular forces (with emphasis on airpower), with UMT as a useful addition to the regular establishment but hardly a substitute for it. The questions of the comparative democratic qualities of UMT versus a large regular force, and the monetary savings of the War Department alternative to a large regular establishment, were incidental to the major question of how the nation might best be prepared to resist external aggression.

There were certainly some parochial considerations involved in the growing AAF antipathy to UMT, but the evidence points to a real concern on the part of the AAF that a regular military establishment

15. Marshall's June 1945 testimony before the Woodrum Committee, U.S. House, Select Committee on Postwar Military Policy, *Hearings*, 79th Cong., 1st sess., 1945, p. 570.
16. Stimson's testimony before Woodrum Committee, 1945, pp. 479–86.

(Army plus Air Force) of 275,000 troops would not meet the anticipated needs of national defense.

> Under the only basis for planning now approved in the War Department our ready combat force in the air would be about 16 groups, or less than 1000 aircraft. Such a token force is disproportionate to our obligations nationally and internationally. Reserve elements cannot be taken as equivalent to a ready M-day force. The overall program envisaged will require a large training establishment. We are in no position to disarm in the air. The American people now have the realization of these matters. We must prepare against sudden aggression.[17]

Parochialism was evident when the Air Force planners anticipated the Navy's usurping the entire airpower mission should the War Department, through extreme self-limitation, provide such a small force that the Navy would propose a large navy and naval air force to ensure the security that the 16-group plan could not offer.

> It seems entirely possible that, if the War Department should develop only the one plan for its peacetime establishment, based on an assumed limitation of a billion-dollar-a-year Regular Army budget (including Air Force), and should it have no other plan to offer when the time comes to submit its recommendations to Congress, the people may well look to the Navy to provide total security in the air, as already advocated by many Navy enthusiasts. Surely it will not be War Department policy that the Navy is to provide the peacetime M-day Air Force. This, to me, could not be accepted as in the best interests of the nation, militarily, politically, or economically.[18]

After March 1945 the PWD continued to plan for the alternative of UMT, since it had planned for this in the past; it was required by the SPD to have an up-to-date plan for a postwar Air Force with the task of training 200,000 trainees, and it still anticipated the possibility that the final force structure would include a combination of the 70 regular groups plus UMT.[19] However, in the eyes of the Air Force planners, UMT was suspect, as was any program, service, or individual that challenged the 70-group program.

The debate between the AAF and the Army over UMT in general lacked the parochialism and counterparochialism evident in the debate over other issues. Although the Air Force eventually took a position of opposition to UMT, during the period prior to March 1945 it officially supported the system which many of its planners and leaders seriously questioned. The Air Force leaders were reluctant to challenge Marshall because they wished to give firm support to his positions in order to reciprocate for his continuing support of Air Force expansion and auton-

17. Memorandum from Arnold to Marshall (30 March 1945), p. 1.
18. *Ibid.*, p. 5.
19. On 2 July 1945, a Universal Military Training branch was established within the Post War Division. DAR, AC/AS–5, 3 July 1945.

omy. Instead of parochialism and counterparochialism, the planners' support of Marshall was an example of mutual respect and admiration. There was no negotiation on this issue, and the support given was not on a *quid pro quo* basis; rather, it was a generous act based on the mutual good will that Marshall and the Air Force leaders had created through the years.

The case made earlier that Air Force parochialism was largely a reaction to the fancied narrow thinking of Army and Navy leaders finds some reinforcement in the UMT debate. Marshall was viewed by the Air Force leaders as an objective man who was almost devoid of favoritism toward a particular service. This view led to an Air Force policy of support for his UMT program despite serious doubts about its efficacy. Although this support ended in March 1945, the cogent question is not why it ended but why it lasted so long. This case illustrates that parochialism could be specific (that is, related to issues and personalities) and not necessarily all-encompassing.

Generals Marshall and Tompkins (Marshall's chief postwar planner) were absolutely convinced of the necessity of a UMT program for all young men in the postwar United States. Since Marshall was convinced that it was essential, he was sure that Congress would agree and that UMT would become a reality. Marshall's perception of what Congress would and would not accept in the postwar period had a considerable influence on the War Department's postwar planning. Based on his prewar experience with Congress, Marshall assumed that it would not accept a large regular establishment, a large defense budget, or a system of selective service. Marshall's 1945 testimony before the Woodrum Committee is illustrative of his thinking.

> Unless you have lived through the parsimonious peacetime attitude you do not realize how determining is the factor of military costs, and what are the probabilities of maintaining, from year to year, your planned estab- ᾽ lishment.
>
> I frequently hear the comment, "We have learned our lesson." I don't believe we have.
>
> I am convinced that when the Congress finds itself approaching a great political campaign with the Budget, of necessity, a major factor, then the Army is in deep trouble, inevitably, and unless the structure we now erect is built to meet that inevitable situation, our best resolutions today won't amount to much for the future.[20]

Curiously, Marshall's experience with the post-World War I defeat by Congress of a universal training program did not seem to cause him any concern over congressional opposition to a peacetime UMT program in the post-World War II period. Marshall's earlier experience probably convinced him that one way to persuade the American people and the

20. Marshall's testimony before Woodrum Committee. U.S. House of Representatives, Select Committee on Postwar Military Policy, *Hearings*, 79th Cong., 1st sess., 1945, pp. 575–76.

Congress of the need for UMT was for the military to present a unified position, rather than the post-World War I split position which resulted from the conflicting viewpoints and personalities of Generals March and Pershing. The fact that the Chief of Staff of the Army in the immediate post-World War I period had advocated a large professional army and had little interest in UMT had made the task of convincing Congress of the efficacy of UMT most difficult for General Pershing, Colonel Marshall, and Colonel John M. Palmer.[21]

Alternative planning to insure that plans existed for both a military structure bolstered by a UMT program and one without such a program was not accomplished by the War Department in the 1943–45 period. An alternate plan was constructed by the AAF after the leaders had become convinced of the ineffectiveness and probable rejection by Congress of a UMT program.[22]

The AAF and the Army approaches to a military establishment without UMT were considerably different. Marshall, despite his reluctance to envision the postwar United States without UMT, considered that the only alternative to it was a large military establishment. The AAF estimated that the postwar Air Force with no UMT would be smaller by 250,000 men than one with it. Since the number of trainees for the Air Force had consistently been considered to be 200,000, and since a training cadre of about 50,000 would be required to administer the AAF portion of the UMT program, it is evident that the AAF postwar planners contemplated UMT as an addition to, but in no way a substitute for, regular air forces. In Moffat's words:

> It is believed that the Air Force should be ready with two plans independent of War Department plans; one with Universal Military Training, the other without Universal Military Training. Although positive figures can not be given at this time, it is estimated that the total strength of the Air Forces on active duty with UMT should be about three quarters of a million; without UMT but making a maximum use of civilians, it should be something over a half million.[23]

The War Department Budget Office attempted to accomplish alternative planning by designing two budget estimates, one based on a regular army of 981,237 with UMT, and another based on a regular army of 2,776,733 with no UMT. General Richards, the War Department Budget Officer, attempted what was not tried by the SPD: planning for alternatives based on the supposition that the UMT program was not an inevitability. Within a month of this attempt, Marshall not only had rejected the idea of alternative planning but also had seriously

21. Forrest C. Pogue, *George C. Marshall: Education of a General, 1880–1939* (New York: Viking Press, 1963), pp. 203–10.

22. The postwar planners' UMT program was simply an addendum to their plans for the regular establishment.

23. Letter from Moffat to AC/AS-1. Subject: Post-War Personnel Plans (24 July 1945). 145.96–128 (111-M-B); 8090–32.

questioned planning without consideration of budgetary limitations. Richards had seen his role of budget officer as a coordinator of military requirements. He desired to defer to "the President and the interested Committee of Congress"[24] for decisions on any budgetary limitations that might be necessary. The similarity of perspective of the War Department Budget Office and that of the AAF Post War Division was short-lived. In November 1944, Marshall made it clear to Richards that his approach was in error and that budgetary considerations would be the determining factor in the calculation of force structures rather than estimates of the national security needs which were evident in Richards' basic assumptions.[25]

Marshall, who had been in Washington for the first five years after World War I, was aware of what had happened to the March-Baker Plan for an Army of 500,000 men. By a process of annual cutbacks in force levels, the U.S. Army was diminished to such a point that by the mid-1920's there was neither a large military establishment nor UMT. Marshall was philosophically opposed to large regular forces, economically conservative in his approach to federal spending, and absolutely convinced that Congress and the people would not accept a large military establishment. The SPD, in conjunction with Marshall's wishes, rejected suggestions by some War Department leaders and planners that a plan, based on the strong possibility that UMT might be rejected by Congress, was needed.[26]

Marshall realized that technological progress was rapidly diminishing the protection afforded the United States by sea and arctic barriers; he did not, however, believe that the fundamental attitudes of the United States citizenry had changed as a result of the increasing strategic vulnerability of the United States. Yet he was willing to assume that the people would accept UMT. Marshall's directive to the SPD on 13 November 1944 indicates his appreciation of the strategic results of World War II.

> I wish that the entire matter of post-war strengths be re-surveyed, having strictly in mind the debilitation of the Axis powers, the huge resources for a long period of years that we shall possess in the form of Army and Navy materiel, and in vastly increased power which will be given us by an annual program of universal military training—something we have never previously enjoyed.[27]

24. WDSBO (War Department Special Budget Office) 111 Postwar (10-4-44). Subject: Estimates for Post War Military Establishment (4 October 1944), p. 1. 145.86–40; 4334–16.

25. *Ibid.*, pp. 1–2.

26. At a 24 November 1944 meeting to re-survey postwar strengths, Colonel Blair of the U.S. Army suggested the composition of such a plan. Colonel Textor, Assistant Director of the Special Planning Division, rejected the idea (25 November 1944), p. 2. 145.86–57; 4334–139.

27. Quoted in a 17 November 1944 memorandum from Kuter to the Chief of the Air Staff. 145.86–29; 4334–206.

Marshall, looking objectively at the postwar world, saw no real danger that might require large regular forces. The U.S. was certainly more vulnerable to attack than it had been prior to the advent of long-range aircraft, but Marshall, in late 1944, evinced little concern about American security largely because he could envisage no enemy, now that the Axis powers were being defeated. General Handy, Marshall's Deputy Chief of Staff and long-time associate, reflected Marshall's thinking when at a 16 November 1944 meeting he advanced certain ideas for consideration.

   a. There will be a National Guard.
   b. The number of regular soldiers must be held to the lowest practicable limit.
   c. Ideas as to what constitutes a balanced force must be adjusted to peacetime conditions. Soldiers in peace are not fighting and must do some of the work which would be provided for them in time of war. Balance between air forces and ground forces is determined by other things, but balance as between combat and service troops should be calculated on 1944 figures.[28]

The concern among the Army leaders was how to keep the troops busy and how to limit the regular establishment.[29] There was little concern shown by either Handy or Marshall about immediate postwar dangers to the security of the United States. The contrast between Army and Air Force thinking was considerable at this time and throughout the entire 1943–45 period. The Air Force leaders and planners anticipated danger in every direction and saw the need for a vast overseas complex of bases with a strategic-bombardment capability to strike anywhere in the world on short notice. Marshall saw debilitated Axis powers, while the AAF leaders and planners feared resurgence of the same.

28. *Ibid.* The difference between Handy's figure of 105 groups which he recommended to the AAF in 1943 and this position in 1944 can be explained by the fact that the figure of 105 groups was to be used for the "interim" period following the war.

29. "The mission of the War Department during the period immediately following V-J Day is stated as follows:

   a. To demobilize the Army and eliminate and curtail the activities of the War Department to the maximum extent and with the greatest rapidity consistent with national commitments for occupational forces.

   b. To provide the occupational forces in liberated areas with sufficient trained personnel, supplies and equipment to assure the proper performance of their missions and to assure their maintenance at standards befitting American soldiers.

   c. To make reasonable provisions for fundamental postwar military requirements. Such provisions must not interfere with demobilization and the elimination and curtailment of War Department activities."

Memorandum from Marshall to Commanding Generals, ASF, AGF, and AAF, and all War Department General and Special Staff Divisions. Subject: War Department Policies for the period following V-J Day (15 August 1945), p. 1. 145.86–100; 2–2210–15.

The War Department postwar planning lagged considerably behind that of the AAF; and in many cases it was the AAF planners who prodded the War Department into making decisions (with regard to the postwar military) which would assist the AAF planners in the assumptions they drew. Kuter's interest in postwar planning and Arnold's toleration of it were both basically motivated by parochialism. The War Department planners, lacking any such motivation, did not have either the personal incentive or the interest of the Army leadership to cause them to accelerate the postwar planning process. In answer to a question about the size of the postwar establishment asked of Marshall by Representative Bulwinkle in July 1945, Marshall said, "Mr. Bulwinkle, I won't attempt to answer that right now. I am very much in the dark. You cannot determine that until we know the character of the peace. I am referring to the Active Army."[30]

The assumption made by the SPD of either twelve or eighteen months between victory in Europe and victory in the Pacific made no great urgency for planning (prior to V-E Day) for the peacetime period. Army postwar planning was not divided into two parts as was the case in the AAF. The SPD of the War Department Special Staff was required to plan for redeployment of forces from Europe to Japan, for demobilization, and for postwar War Department organization, force levels, and base requirements. The immediate problems so occupied the SPD that much of the detailed planning for the postwar period was deferred to the time between V-E and V-J Days—a period officially estimated in October 1944 to be eighteen months[31] but which, of course, lasted only about four.

The dissimilar philosophies of the War Department and the AAF concerning peacetime military forces, their different perceptions of postwar dangers to United States national security, the fundamental dichotomy of views concerning the strategic warning the United States would have before an enemy attack, and the differences between the training requirements of the Army and those of the AAF, all contributed to the opposing attitudes of the two groups over UMT that emerged as the war drew to a close.

The postwar debate which took place in the press and Congress, though of considerable intensity and occasional erudition, never focused on the question of what was needed for national defense. UMT had met with ignominious death by 1948, but its defeat was not because of its irrelevance in an age of airpower, nuclear weapons, and exploding technology, but because of the fundamental antipathy of the majority of

30. U.S. House of Representatives, Select Committee on Postwar Military Policy, *Hearings*, 79th Cong., 1st sess., 1945, p. 575.
31. Memorandum for Deputy Chief of Staff, U.S. Army. Subject: Changes in Definitions as to duration of demobilization and Post-War Planning Periods, from Major General Tompkins (2 October 1944). 145.86–257; 4334–139. The earlier estimate of twelve months from V-E to V-J Days was changed to eighteen months in this memorandum with no explanation given of the rationale for this change.

Americans to military service in peacetime. Although this antipathy was not evident in the opinion polls taken in the immediate postwar period, support for the program in general did not mean support for the program when it involved sending relatives and friends to a year of military training.

8

Bargaining at the Periphery: Anti-Aircraft Artillery and Air Liaison

The question of autonomy for the postwar Air Force was not a clear issue in the sense that there were certain missions which logically could be placed within two or more services. The strategic bombardment mission was what the AAF leaders used to justify autonomy, yet they wished to place a number of other missions under the new, separate air force: tactical aviation, air defense, transport aviation, anti-aircraft artillery, land-based anti-submarine aviation, basic military aviation training, liaison aviation, and air engineers (for air field construction). There evolved a contest between Army and AAF planners and leaders for two of these missions which were on the periphery of the fundamental issue of an independent military airpower capability: anti-aircraft artillery and air liaison.[1] The bargaining that took place over these two missions gives further insight into both the ordering of priorities by the AAF postwar planners and their doctrinal focus.

Although the extreme protagonists for a separate Air Force with all airpower under its command considered these peripheral missions terribly important, the order of priorities for every identifiable voice within the AAF was autonomy first (with strategic bombardment inextricably tied to autonomy), followed by tactical aviation, air defense, air transportation, and other missions in some descending order of priority.

The final outcome was the failure of the United States Air Force, which was established in 1947, to gain exclusive control over basic military aviation training, liaison aircraft, air engineers, anti-aircraft artillery, or land-based anti-submarine aviation. In fact, in 1947 the Air Force received no air engineers (the Army Corps of Engineers was given the responsibility for airbase construction), no anti-aircraft artillery, and no land-based anti-submarine aviation. The Army retained its liaison aircraft, the engineering mission, and anti-aircraft artillery; and the Navy, the training responsibility for all its aviation as well as the anti-submarine mission (both land- and sea-based). The Air Force did receive strategic aviation, tactical aviation, air-defense aviation, and transport aviation, though exclusive control of each of these missions eluded it since the Navy and Marines were potential competitors in each of these areas, as was the Army in tactical aviation. Anti-aircraft artillery and air liaison invite particular attention, for they were two peripheral missions which were used as bargaining points by the postwar planners. The result of the bargaining process which took place in the summer and autumn of 1945

1. Light aircraft used in the battlefield area for artillery spotting, inter-unit communication, observation, and transportation are liaison aircraft. This military mission is called air liaison.

gives further insights into the variance in parochialism among AAF leaders.

During the interwar period the Army Air Corps had neglected air liaison as a result of extreme budgetary limitations and a greater interest in the more sophisticated combat planes.[2] When funds for aircraft procurement became available between 1939 and 1941, Army Air Corps leaders and procurement officers continued to neglect the liaison mission. This neglect resulted from three factors. Despite authorization for large numbers of aircraft, the AAF was faced with an American aircraft industry burdened with the task of supplying aircraft to the British (and by mid-1941 to the Russians), trying to meet the demands of quantity and tight time schedules of the Army Air Corps and the United States Navy, and simultaneously attempting to expand enormously its production capability with all the construction and training delays that expansion entailed.[3] The second factor that inhibited development and production of liaison aircraft between 1939 and 1941 was the doctrinal focus of Air Corps leaders which caused them to order their priorities in both interest and aircraft procurement in such a manner that bombardment, transport, pursuit, and attack aircraft all had a higher priority than liaison aircraft.[4] The third inhibiting factor was the absence of large Army maneuvers in the 1920's and 1930's; this lack (until 1940) made the need for great numbers of liaison aircraft in the battlefield area mainly a matter of conjecture. Although the Army Air Corps leadership had relied heavily on theory to justify the strategic bombardment mission in the interwar period, it was unwilling to accept the theory of Army ground officers concerning the need for liaison aircraft on the modern battlefield.[5]

The Army, frustrated in its attempts to convince the Air Corps that it should procure in quantity liaison aircraft that were easy to maintain, could land on unimproved airstrips, and had the necessary communications equipment on board to facilitate command and control as well as artillery spotting and control, decided to rent commercial light aircraft for its 1941 maneuvers.[6] The maneuvers convinced the Army ground leaders of the need for light aircraft to be assigned to and controlled by the Army commander in the field.[7] Throughout World War II the general practice was for light aircraft to be assigned directly to Army units.

2. I. B. Holley, *Evolution of the Liaison-Type Airplane: 1917–1944* (Washington: AAF Historical Office, AAF Historical Studies No. 44, 1946), chaps. II–VII.

3. Wesley F. Craven and James L. Cate, eds., *The Army Air Forces in World War II* (Chicago: University of Chicago Press, 1955), Vol. VI, chap. IX.

4. "Unfortunately, the delay in procuring light airplanes in quantity led the ground forces to overemphasize the Air Corps' unwillingness to cooperate and consequently to stress the necessity of organic observation aviation within the ground arms." Holley, *Liaison-Type Airplane*, p. 81.

5. Army Air Corps leaders also doubted the survival ability in a battle area of a slow, unarmed plane. Craven and Cate, *The Army Air Forces*, Vol. VI, p. 222.

6. Holley, *Liaison-Type Airplane*, p. 92.

7. *Ibid.*, p. 97.

The PWD wrestled with the problem of liaison aircraft from the summer of 1943 until the autumn of 1944 without reaching any decision;[8] to justify liaison aircraft exclusively under the control of a separate Air Force was difficult because of the need for ground commander control of observation, spotting, and organic liaison aircraft.

The PWD decided to have a comprehensive study made of liaison aviation, and an artillery officer, Lieutenant Colonel Robert R. Williams, was selected by Moffat to undertake it. Williams made an extensive trip through the various combat areas in Europe and interviewed many Army and AAF commanders in the field. On 8 September 1945 Williams submitted his report to Moffat, in which he recommended that the Army retain its organic liaison aircraft in the postwar period.[9] Moffat approved this study (as did Norstad), but Generals F. H. Smith, Jr., and Hoyt S. Vandenberg had reservations about assigning this mission to the Army, fearing that the Army would convert these aircraft into light, close-support fighter bombers and into light airlift aircraft, and that it would eventually usurp the tactical airlift and close support missions.[10]

The AAF leadership faced a dilemma on this issue in that an official AAF study had recommended liaison aircraft for the Army and the Army leaders were aware of this study. The practice in wartime was to have liaison aircraft permanently assigned to the ground units. General Norstad not only accepted the recommendations of the study but sincerely believed that the Army needed "organic" liaison aircraft. Thus the AAF-Army contest for liaison aircraft was lost before there was an engagement. Colonel Moffat, in an attempt to be objective, had engaged a ground officer to do the study. The danger of such fairness was that the study might recommend something other than what was desired by most AAF leaders; this was precisely the result.

Air liaison of the battlefield area became an Army mission as a result of three factors: neglect in the 1920's and 1930's (especially in the late 1930's) of the liaison requirement of an increasingly mobile Army by Air Corps leadership; the commissioning and acceptance of the Williams study; and the continued AAF doctrinal focus which caused postwar planners to consider ground forces and affiliated missions largely obsolescent. Norstad's initial reaction to the effect on future warfare of the technological breakthrough in weaponry which the atomic bomb entailed is indicative of the various forms of weaponry and tactics which

8. The 105-group plan called for artillery-control and liaison aircraft to be an Army responsibility. 105-group plan, p. 4. The 78-group plan stated: "... there will be a requirement for trained Air Force personnel to serve the ground forces, under Army command, for artillery spotting." 78-group plan, p. 3.

9. 145.86–58; 4334–188.

10. Norstad countered the Smith and Vandenberg criticism of his approval of the findings of this study by indicating that he was "going along" with the previously announced AAF policy (as stated in a disposition form). Subject: "Organic Assignment of Aircraft other than to the Air Forces," from Deputy Commander, AAF, to G-3 (10 October 1944). Norstad memorandum to Chief of Air Staff (4 January 1946). 145.86–58; 4334–198.

AAF leadership considered obsolescent or obsolete in the late summer and autumn of 1945. "Although the conception of a tactical air force was one of the greatest developments of this war, it is now as old-fashioned as the Maginot Line. Ground warfare will take place, if any [*sic*], 18 months after a settlement of peace, by occupational forces." [11]

The AAF relinquished the anti-aircraft artillery mission for rather different reasons than those evident in the case of air liaison, though the important doctrinal factor was substantially the same. Anti-aircraft artillery had developed slowly in the interwar period as a branch of the Coast Artillery Corps of the United States Army. The Army Air Corps leadership throughout the twenties and thirties considered anti-aircraft artillery an ineffective weapon against aerial attack for a number of reasons. The difficulty in aiming at, tracking, and hitting high-flying maneuverable aircraft was acknowledged by the Air Corps and Coast Artillery Corps leaders alike; the retarded development of radar in the United States made destruction of aircraft by anti-aircraft artillery virtually impossible in bad weather when attackers could not be seen by anti-aircraft gunners; [12] the ability of aircraft to approach targets from many altitudes and directions made defending a single target difficult. To the critics of anti-aircraft artillery the defense of many targets seemed an insuperable problem. Nevertheless, the Coast Artillery Corps, finding it increasingly difficult to defend its primary mission of coastline defense through the use of long-range coast artillery cannon, accelerated the development of anti-aircraft artillery in the late 1930's.

The anti-aircraft artillery mission, which before World War II had been exclusively under Army control, came gradually under AAF control as the war progressed. [13] The reason for this was that its main function was air-base defense. [14] Air-base defense was a coordinated effort of defensive fighters, anti-aircraft artillery, searchlight batteries, and radar and visual reconnaissance. The anti-aircraft artillery commander was a ground officer (Coast Artillery Corps) who was under the operational command of the air defense commander, an air officer. [15]

11. A directive given to Colonel Cole by General Norstad, quoted in a memorandum for Colonel Moffat from Colonel Cole. Subject: A Realistic Conception of a Post-War Air Force (22 August 1945). 4334–206.

12. Use of sonics to track unseen aircraft was only partially successful.

13. A wartime intraservice rivalry was evident on the issue of control of anti-aircraft artillery. The Army Air Force, by April 1944, had generally won its case for operational control of AAA. C. L. Grant, *AAF Air Defense Activities in the Mediterranean: 1942–1944* (Maxwell AFB, Ala.: USAF Historical Division, USAF Historical Study No. 66, 1954), chap. IV.

14. "When anti-aircraft artillery, searchlights, and barrage balloons operate in the air defense of the same areas with aviation, the efficient exploitation of the special capabilities of each, and the avoidance of unnecessary losses to friendly aviation, demand that all be placed under the command of the air commander responsible for the area." Field Manual 100–20, par. 18b, quoted in memorandum to the PWD from Major General Oldfield, Special Assistant for AAA (30 May 1945). 1.145.86–70; 4334–167.

15. Grant, *Activities in the Mediterranean.*

All the AAF postwar plans included the anti-aircraft artillery within the autonomous postwar Air Force; Major General Barney Old-field, Arnold's special assistant for AAA, on numerous occasions during the 1943–45 period recommended the incorporation of AAA within the postwar Air Force.   In a memorandum to Arnold, Oldfield said:

> To insure protection required for our air installations it is mandatory that the antiaircraft defenses provided therefore be an integral part of the Air Force.   This will guarantee the proper strategic development of all means of air defense under one responsible commander and will provide the unity of command required for prompt and decisive action, both defensively and offensively, on M-day.[16]

Yet by the end of 1945 the AAF leadership had rather gracefully conceded this mission to the Army, as indicated by a memorandum from Tompkins to Arnold.   The assumption that anti-aircraft artillery would be a postwar Air Force function was not the War Department position.   "As for the position of Anti-Aircraft Artillery, it was shown under ground forces in the War Department Post-War Troop Basis, since that is its (the War Department's) present position."[17]

A primary reason for conceding this mission, which may not be self-evident, was the dual problem of the "non-rated" officer and officer seniority.   It was generally accepted throughout the AAF that a non-flyer should not be placed in command of any AAF unit whose primary mission was military aviation.[18]   Incorporation of anti-aircraft artillery into the Air Force would limit the career possibilities of talented anti-aircraft artillery officers, who, as non-flyers, could not expect to reach the top positions of leadership within the postwar Air Force.[19]   A coordinate problem concerned the many senior officers within the Coast Artillery Corps whom the AAF leadership was reluctant to assimilate into a service that valued youth and vigor among its second-echelon leaders.   The anticipated result of such an incorporation was large-scale demotion for the youthful AAF generals, with the older, more senior (but often less high-ranking) anti-aircraft artillery officers retaining their wartime rank.   The morale problem was twofold: anti-aircraft artillery officers

16. Memorandum for the Air Staff, Plans, from Oldfield.   Subject: Tentative Estimated Anti-Aircraft Requirements for Post-War Planning (15 November 1943), p. 1.   145.041A–19; 2–2141–73B.

17. Memorandum to Arnold from Tompkins.   Subject: Expansion of the Outline of the Post-War Military Establishment (13 September 1944), p. 2.   145.86–29; 4334–206.

18. Approximately 15,000 AAA officers were to be integrated into a postwar Air Force officer corps of approximately 80,000 officers exclusive of AAA officers.

19. "It is my opinion that in the recent expansion of the AAF, the non-rated officer has not been unduly discriminated against."   Memorandum for General Vandenberg from Brigadier General A. R. Maxwell, Chief, Requirements Division, AC/AS–3.   Subject: Career for Non-rated Officers in Regular Establishment (26 October 1945).   1.145.86–88; 4631–76.   General Maxwell suggests, by using the word "unduly," that there was discrimination.

would consider their military careers limited because of their lack of flying experience; AAF officers would resent the influx of large numbers of officers of high rank into a promotion system already strained by the postwar curtailment of many wartime general officer billets.   Thus, aside from any doctrinal or organizational rationale concerning the inclusion or exclusion of anti-aircraft artillery within the postwar Air Force, there were morale considerations which were weighed seriously by the postwar planners.

Kuter, who was absolutely convinced that air defense could be performed effectively and efficiently only if all elements of air defense were assigned to one service—the Air Force, was unwilling to accept morale considerations as a valid reason for the continuance of anti-aircraft artillery as a function of the Army.[20]   Norstad, however, considering the arrangement of air-base defense satisfactory as it had evolved during the war, concerned about morale considerations, and aware that the incorporation of anti-aircraft artillery into the postwar Air Force would entail a diminishing number of aircraft groups, was willing to relinquish the anti-aircraft artillery mission to retain the 70-group Air Force.[21] The incorporation of anti-aircraft artillery might not have doomed the 70-group Air Force, but some of those 70 groups would have been anti-aircraft artillery groups.

In the summer and autumn of 1945, when the postwar planners were attempting to cut back on all nonessential missions in order to retain a large military airpower capability, the anti-aircraft artillery and air liaison (as well as air engineer) missions were considered important but not essential parts of the overall Air Force mission.   They became the bargaining points which the AAF planners used to get support from the Army for autonomy and the 70-group Air Force.

Doctrine, which was such an important factor in all AAF postwar planning, had a role to play in the ordering of priorities.   Air liaison, anti-aircraft artillery, and air engineers were all rather incidental to the strategic bombardment mission.   To save the full complement of bombardment and long-range fighter groups, the peripheral missions were rather courteously surrendered to the Army by General Norstad. By taking a firm position, Norstad might have retained the 70-group Air Force as well as the peripheral missions which were relinquished to the Army.   Norstad and W. Stuart Symington, Assistant Secretary of War for Air from January 1946 until unification, were not willing to take an uncompromising position because they needed Army support for autonomy and the 70-group program.[22]   In addition, Norstad and a number of other AAF leaders never considered these peripheral missions ones that could be carried out only under Air Force command

20. Kuter interview.
21. Norstad interview.
22. Alfred Goldberg, ed., *A History of the United States Air Force, 1907–1957* (Princeton: Van Nostrand, 1957), p. 155.

and control.[23]   The essentially nonparochial Norstad has been criticized for his lack of toughness and stubbornness in intraservice and interservice infighting in the immediate postwar period, but it was less a case of his being outfought for these missions by Army protagonists than of his sincere belief that the missions could be carried out just as well by the Army.   Air Force autonomy and the 70-group Air Force were Norstad's primary aims; and he, as well as the Air Force leadership, displayed considerable toughness when these goals were threatened in the postwar period.

23. Among the AAF leaders who felt Norstad's position on anti-aircraft artillery was correct were George, Giles, Cabell, and Spaatz.   Those opposed to compromise were Kuter and Fred Anderson.

9

Conclusion

The AAF planners at the operational planning level did not like to mix domestic political considerations with military considerations. Their reasoning was that the conduct of warfare was a military matter and that the inclusion of political considerations was likely to delay or confuse the accomplishment of military victory.[1] In the area of postwar planning, however, the AAF planners were aware that military planning had to be in keeping with the foreign policy of the United States and that a military structure had to be designed which would give the government the necessary military instruments to carry out its foreign policies.

Since the planners could not accurately anticipate American postwar foreign policy and since they were reluctant to confer with State Department officials to gain insights into the possible policy problems of the postwar world, they decided to design a force which would be so large that it could handle every conceivable contingency.[2] The figure of 105 groups which General Handy had suggested as a force level for the immediate postwar period was eagerly grasped by the planners, since it was a figure that would make possible an enormous postwar air force and since it was received from a high-ranking Army officer. The 105-group plan, together with its deployment schedule, was considered by the planners a force of sufficient size to establish a *Pax Americana* throughout half the world (the Western Hemisphere and the Pacific). Combined with the British military force, an American postwar Air Force of 105 groups would be large enough to police the entire world.[3]

1. "Since our return, in addition to catching up with the normal, rapid flow of events, there has been an extremely heavy session between the British and American Chiefs, and between the President and the Prime Minister over future operations in the Mediterranean. That issue, has, however, been settled to the complete satisfaction of the U.S. Chiefs. It is a most reassuring example of solidarity and unity between the military and political interests on the American side in contrast with the British side, in which we believe the political interest took over and dominated the military." Letter from Kuter to Norstad (5 July 1944), p. 1. 145.81–80; 2930–39.

2. Correspondingly, there was a reluctance on the part of the State Department to make policy forecasts. Interviews with Tompkins and Davison.

3. The AAF postwar planners were not the only men in Washington who envisaged the postwar role of the United States military as the world's policeman. "I personally believe that a nation blessed as this nation is with everything that it takes in manpower and material resources to be powerful in a military way has it within its own control, if it wants to do it, to see to it there is no more war." Secretary of War Robert Patterson's testimony, U.S. House of Representatives, Committee on Military Affairs, *Hearings on H.R. 515*, 79th Congress, 1st sess., 1945, p. 58. "It is my personal opinion that the greatest single motivating force for world peace today is the organized military potential of the United States. . . ." General of the Army Dwight D. Eisenhower's testimony, *ibid.*, p. 61.

Conclusion

National defense and defense of the Western Hemisphere were mentioned as two important goals which would require military forces, but there is no question that the sights of the postwar planners extended considerably beyond these limits. The desired force level of 105 groups, deployed to distant places and concentrating heavily on strategic bombardment, was a formidable structure which considerably exceeded any requirement for defense, even considering the fact that the Western Hemisphere and the American possessions in the Pacific did represent a large geographic area to be defended.

The postwar planners faced a technological, industrial, and administrative dilemma which they felt could be solved in only one way: through the maintenance of a large regular postwar Air Force. The experience of World War II offered certain lessons. The production of aircraft in quantity was impossible without the existence of a large, modern aircraft industry prior to the commencement of hostilities. Training of aircrews was an extremely long process that required extensive training facilities, competent flying instructors, a small instructor-to-student ratio, and a period of twenty months just to produce a novice combat pilot. In addition, the planners were plagued by the problem of maintaining proficiency in combat aircraft. Building air bases to include runways, hangars, housing facilities, gasoline storage and refueling facilities, communications, lighting, and ramp and parking facilities was a costly and lengthy job; with the increasing weight and size of aircraft, future problems would dwarf the considerable wartime problems in air base construction.

A small regular postwar Air Force could not train and give operational experience to the enormous numbers of reserve pilots who would be needed to meet the requirement of having a 1.5-million-man operational Air Force one year after mobilization. Such was the size of the force included in the various War Department strategic assumptions of the 1944 period.[4]

A small regular Air Force in combination with commercial aviation was unlikely to require sufficient airplanes to insure a large, advanced aircraft industry which could produce combat aircraft in quantity in time of national emergency. A small postwar Air Force would not need large numbers of modern air bases both within the United States and abroad to supply the air-base requirements in time of rapid mobilization and deployment. A small regular Air Force might not withstand the initial attack of an enemy, and the war might be lost with the destruction of United States airpower in the early stages of conflict. The postwar planners, trying to determine the force level needed to avoid vulnerability to attack, found the small, 16-group Air Force that remained within the budget ceilings established by General Marshall not only inadequate to meet the needs of national defense but a possible invitation for a quick, devastating blow from any potential enemy.

4. V-J plan, p. 6. Also 29 March 1945 chart.

Of all the considerations that appeared to the planners to justify a large Air Force in the first few years after World War II, the maintenance of a modern aircraft industrial plant was probably the most important single factor. The planners anticipated a period of years in the postwar world during which surplus military cargo and transport aircraft could fill most of the commercial aircraft requirements. The planners feared that this factor, combined with the small need for aircraft that a small postwar Air Force would have, would idle such a great portion of the aircraft industry that within a few years that industry would lose its ability to produce aircraft rapidly to meet a national emergency. A large regular Air Force, which was given the necessary funds to keep modernizing its force, would allow an aviation industry of moderate size to withstand the first years of low commercial aviation demand and to enter the decade of the 1950's with a technologically advanced production capability. Here is a rather different view of the "military-industrial" complex, for instead of industry insisting on a large air force, the AAF planners were insisting on a large aircraft industry to insure that the anticipated mobilization and developmental needs in military aviation could be met by the aircraft industry.

General Arnold believed—and the postwar planners were in complete agreement with him—that as long as the United States maintained its technological lead in aviation, in general, and in strategic bombardment, in particular, there would be little to fear from any potential aggressor. The technological focus which characterized the postwar planning process made the prospect of a moth-balled aircraft industry most unattractive. The planners recognized that only an aircraft industry that was actively working on developments in aviation technology could insure that the United States would maintain its technological lead over other states. To quote from the V-J plan:

> Aircraft production after V-J day is planned on the basis of three primary considerations:
>
> (1) To provide aircraft necessary to equip and support the seventy-eight groups in the occupational forces and strategic reserve and to perform the required training functions of the AAF.
>
> (2) To provide the continuity of production essential to maintain an aircraft industry capable of rapid expansion in an emergency.
>
> (3) To introduce new and radically improved models as soon as they have been tested and proved in order to preserve AAF superiority in design and performance.[5]

The technological perspective of the planners, the doctrinal bias that colored the thinking of the AAF leaders in Washington during the planning period, and the importance of autonomy to these leaders explains the motivational considerations endemic to the postwar planning

5. V-J plan, p. 48.

process. The men involved did not consider the identification of post-war enemies, the efficacy of an international organization, and the foreign policy goals of the United States irrelevant; but they considered these factors of secondary importance. First priority throughout the entire planning period went to the creation of an independent air force, second to none in size, technological advancement, and strategic capability. If this goal could be accomplished, the planners were sure that no matter what political situation the United States might face it would have the necessary military forces to carry out its policies.

Postwar planning within the Air Force was initiated for parochial reasons, and during the two-year planning period, the goal of autonomy was never forgotten. Yet the planning went considerably beyond the parochial. The planners posited certain assumptions in order to justify a large postwar air force, and a superficial view of the record might result in the conclusion that this period was another prosaic example of unproductive interservice rivalry. The messianic quality of the AAF doctrine indicates that despite the parochial motivations which led to the creation of the PWD, the planners sincerely believed in the maintenance of earthly peace through American airpower. The roles of ground and sea power were deprecated not out of a fundamental distrust of Army and Navy leaders but because of the postwar planners' conviction that these two services were irrelevant.

The evidence is substantial that the AAF was much more thorough in its postwar planning than was the Army in that it created in the 1943–45 period a number of plans based on different sets of assumptions, while the Army planned largely on the basis of one set of assumptions. The AAF planners had a plan that included UMT, and one without it; a plan that assumed an effective international organization, and one that assumed no such organization; a study based on a year's warning before war, and one for little or no warning.

The Army assumptions were that UMT would be accepted by Congress and the American public, that Congress would not accept a large regular force, that the regular military forces would be filled by volunteers only, that the number of young men desiring to volunteer for regular military service would be small, and that the international organization would be effective. These assumptions made by General Marshall and the reluctance of the SPD to make alternative plans were based on two factors. Marshall had been so effective in the 1944–45 period in getting his ideas accepted by the President and Congress that the SPD saw no need to doubt that he would be successful in his quest for UMT. Marshall so dominated the Army Staff in Washington during the war that it did not occur to the SPD to be creative and provide him with alternative plans. General Tompkins and his staff, planning on the basis of Marshall's assumptions, attempted to arrive at the best possible force structure consistent with them.

The danger of having such an effective leader as Marshall within the military bureaucracy is that staff creativity slowly erodes in the presence of an admired, intelligent, and persuasive leader. Marshall admired independent thought and creativity, and he received a great deal of both from the semi-independent AAF, from the field, and from a few extremely competent and self-assured staff officers in the War Department. But the great sweep of his intelligence and influence was overpowering to many of his staff officers;[6] the result was a dedicated staff who faithfully carried out his orders and ideas but who failed to present the alternative solutions to postwar problems which might have broadened the scope of War Department postwar planning.

The AAF postwar planning did not suffer from this deficiency. The AAF planners were removed somewhat from Marshall, and General Arnold did not dominate his staff as Marshall tended to do. Arnold, being mostly concerned with operations and a planner only in his awareness of technological changes, exercised less immediate control over the Air Staff, Plans, than over the other major staff agencies within Headquarters, AAF.[7] Also, Kuter, a man of great self-confidence, was not dominated by any senior officer and was able to isolate his PWD from the subtle domination that inhibits creativity. A good illustration of Kuter's independence was his reply to a request from Arnold that the Air Staff, Plans, change its estimate (summer 1943) that the production of German airplanes was increasing.

> The paper in question is Staff Advice to the Commanders. I cannot subscribe to putting in that paper any advice that cannot be supported. Consequently, this particular paper will not be rewritten in the manner in which you expect.
>
> It is very clearly the prerogative of the Commander to throw the advice away and place any figure he may choose in a command paper.[8]

In addition, the AAF postwar planners were required to base their plans on War Department assumptions which they seriously questioned. Hence, they did some alternative planning based on their own estimates of the postwar situation. Having done a great deal of creative planning prior to the time the Army began to send down specific assumptions, the postwar planners were unwilling to constrain their later planning to the War Department's guidelines. The planners were also aware that an essential part of their responsibility was the creation of plans that would justify Air Force autonomy and that their relationship to the Army was one of competitor rather than subordinate.

The top leadership in the military, for all its rivalry, pettiness, and parochialism, was a closely knit group of old friends. Tompkins, head of the SPD, had been a classmate of Arnold's at Command and General Staff School at Fort Leavenworth. The West Point connections and the

6. Forrest C. Pogue, *George C. Marshall: Ordeal and Hope, 1939–1942* (New York: Viking Press, 1966), pp. 13–14.

7. Kuter interview.

8. 6 August 1943. 168.80–1; 5–2405–4.

Staff School friendships combined with the professional ties to help combat the divisiveness caused by intraservice rivalries. The great war machine of 15,000,000 men was operated by a small group of close friends. The twenty years prior to World War II, despite such well-publicized struggles as the Billy Mitchell trial, was a time of interdependence for this small group of military professionals, assaulted at times by civilian critics for their alleged militarism, their drain on the nation's economy, and their supposed guilt in causing the American entrance into World War I.

The Army Air Force differed from the other two services in that young men reached positions of great responsibility. The Advisory Council, which was Arnold's immediate personal staff, consisted of men ranging in age from twenty-five to forty. Kuter and Norstad were in their thirties when they were major generals in charge of all Air Force planning.[9] This youthful group of extremely bright colonels and generals approached their tasks with great energy and enthusiasm, and, unlike Marshall and Arnold, they could endure great workloads and long hours for extended periods of time. Arnold's health throughout the war was not good; he missed the Yalta Conference because he was convalescing from a mild heart attack.[10] Marshall carefully guarded his health by restricting both his office hours and his after-hours commitments.[11]

The youthfulness of key decision-makers did entail some costs. Most of these second-echelon leaders had not been senior enough prior to World War II to have attended the service staff colleges. Their experience within the Air Force was limited, and few had worked with sister services or other branches of government. Most were West Point graduates and a few were ROTC graduates of civilian colleges or universities. None had any graduate-level academic experience. Generally, political naïveté combined with political idealism to produce a positive attitude among these men toward an international organization. There were only a few men in the AAF who questioned the effectiveness of a United Nations to maintain world peace; Generals Fairchild and Kuter both seriously doubted that such a cooperative international organization could do it. The United Nations enthusiasts had never wrestled intellectually with the failure of the League of Nations to resolve conflict and maintain peace. And even Kuter and Fairchild questioned the U.N. primarily on the basis of their experience with Soviet intransigence and not on the basis of an understanding of the frailties of past international organizations.

Postwar plans never mentioned specific enemies even though, traditionally, United States military contingency planning identified

9. Kuter was a brigadier general when he assumed the position of Assistant Chief of Air Staff, Plans; on 20 February 1944 he was promoted to major general. Kuter Papers, vol. IV, part I, p. 38.
10. Kuter interview.
11. Pogue, *Ordeal and Hope*, p. 11.

them.[12]   This reluctance to name enemies stemmed from the unwritten but widely understood rule that no present ally would be specifically identified as a potential enemy.   (The fear of a leak, in conjunction with an acute awareness of the Russian sensitivity toward unfriendly American acts, precluded any specific mention of the Soviet Union in even a top secret plan.)   Draft studies were drawn up in which specific potential enemies were named, but this listing of states was usually eliminated by the Chief of the PWD, Colonel Moffat.   A second factor, of greater importance, was the widely held belief that the United Nations would prevent aggression anywhere it might manifest itself.

The senior Air Force leaders mistrusted political scientists as unfair critics of military men; the second-echelon AAF leaders were largely unaware of the field of political science and knew no one in the academic world except those in aeronautical engineering.   When faced with the probability of a United Nations Organization, these young men, full of optimism, endorsed it, generally viewing the U.N. as a way to insure American national security.   In the immediate postwar period Norstad was very much interested in having closer contact with the academic community than he had had prior to World War II.   The primary reason behind the desire to establish rapport between the military and civilian intellectuals was not to give the military leadership an opportunity to benefit intellectually from such contact; rather, Norstad felt the military should counter pacifism and anti-militarism by keeping the academic community aware of the need for preparedness.[13]

General Kuter mentioned the need for bases in the northern parts of the United States to defend against a polar attack, yet no plan written by the PWD during his tenure recommended bases in Canada or in the northern portion of the United States.   Curiously, the AAF planned as though the world were flat and a Mercator projection best illustrated the approaches to the United States.   The PWD lacked the educational or aviation background to grasp the strategic impact of long-range bombardment aircraft, and the AAF leaders were too busy to notice the discrepancy in base planning.   The threats from the poles were partially recognized at the leadership level but were not stated clearly enough to be incorporated into the postwar plans.

Breakdown in communication between the PWD and the AAF leaders resulted in the postwar planners not being adequately informed of the suspicions about the Soviet Union held by some of the top men (Kuter, O. A. Anderson, Fairchild, and Cabell).   These suspicions were not communicated in writing because of the implicit ban on such action; they

---

12. Mark S. Watson, *Chief of Staff: Prewar Plans and Preparations, United States Army in World War II: The War Department* (Washington: Historical Division, Department of the Army, 1950).   See also Kent Roberts Greenfield, ed., *Command Decisions* (New York: Harcourt, Brace, 1959), esp. chap. iv. by Louis Morton, "Germany First: The Basic Concept of Allied Strategy in World War II."   Japan and Germany were mentioned as possible enemies in a number of studies.

13. Giffin interview.

were probably relayed verbally but with insufficient force to influence the PWD. Thus, a number of top-echelon men thought in terms of the Soviet danger and assumed that their thinking permeated the AAF staff; in fact it did not, since the PWD was thinking in terms of fighting World War II over again with the same enemies and allies. This breakdown in communication went unnoticed, and as the various plans were completed they were hastily read by AAF leaders who accepted them without seriously questioning a base complex that left the northern great-circle routes exposed and unprotected.

This unrealistic planning for the location of bases indicates a fundamental lack of understanding of the implications of long-range strategic bombardment. A resurgent Japan or Germany, an aggressive Great Britain, China, or Soviet Union, would find the shortest route for a direct attack on the United States across the northern arctic wastelands. The postwar plans all specified that they were based on the assumption of a surprise attack upon the soil of the United States by a major power, yet no consideration was given to a base structure to defend against the shortest air route to the United States by any power in the Northern Hemisphere—the route across the North Pole using great-circle routing. Even if the United States was not the object of a direct attack across the poles but rather of an air attack from aircraft carriers, the need for bases in the northern United States and Canada for retaliatory purposes against any of the industrial powers of the Northern Hemisphere would have been a logical requirement. Kuter, who seemed acutely aware of the future vulnerability of the United States to long-range strategic bombardment, seemed unaware of the likely direction of attack. He stressed defense of the northern frontier of the United States, yet he also felt the U.S. was threatened from the south and needed to defend its southern frontiers. No great power in thousands of years has been located in the Southern Hemisphere, nor was an emergent great power in that area evident in the 1940's, yet no emphasis was given in Air Force planning to danger from the north.

Three questions remain unanswered and perhaps are unanswerable. If the attitude of the masses in America had not been isolationist in the thirties, if the Air Corps Tactical School had been able to espouse openly the offensive role of strategic bombardment, if a test of these theories through large scale, realistic maneuvers had been possible, would the United States have entered World War II with better theory and better aircraft? In turn, would the war have been appreciably shortened if a thorough testing of these theories had been possible? And would the postwar planning have been noticeably different had these tests been possible? Only very tentative answers can be offered to these questions, but in view of actual theory development and in view of the rationale behind prewar and postwar planning, some answers may be forthcoming.

As Chennault has polemically, but correctly, pointed out, a fair test of air defense in the 1930's would have shown the vulnerabilities of bombardment aviation and highlighted the need for the development of long-range escort fighters to defend bomber formations. It is doubtful, however, that a fair test could have been accomplished, for with the extreme limitations on funds, the Army Air Corps would have hesitated to test the vulnerability of bombardment aviation at a time when it was extremely difficult to convince the War Department and Congress of the efficacy of bombardment aircraft that did not have a strategic capability due to range limitations (the B-17). If a test had been conducted without publicity, it is still doubtful that serious investigation into the technological possibilities of long-range escort would have been undertaken, because of fund limitations in research and development and because of the hesitation even to suggest that an escort airplane might be required.

When doctrine becomes dogma, all kinds of counter-dogma signals can be ignored. If the lessons of the Battle of Britain could be ignored, if the high losses in bombardment aircraft whenever they were seriously opposed by German fighters in the early, unescorted daylight raids in 1943 could be discounted, if it took the loss of 60 aircraft on a single mission over Schweinfurt in August 1943 and 60 more over Schweinfurt in October 1943 finally to convince all the Air Corps leaders that unescorted bombardment against defended targets was self-defeating as well as suicidal, then is there any reason to believe that attitudinal changes among the American public and in the War Department would have permitted a different Air Force to develop? The answer has to be a tentative no.

By giving a tentative negative answer to the first question, negative answers to questions two and three necessarily follow. What is presented here is not some vague theory of inevitability but rather an analysis based on motivational and theoretical constructs which were largely divorced from the realities of actual situations and technological and tactical developments.

Coordination between AAF Intelligence and the PWD was almost nonexistent. On rare occasions, the Post War Division would request from the Air Staff, Intelligence, an estimate of postwar problems or an evaluation of Soviet intentions in a particular area of the world. In addition, intelligence reports and letters addressed to other divisions within the Air Staff, Plans, would occasionally reach the PWD, but it received no regular flow of intelligence information. The Air Staff, Intelligence, was in the habit of dealing with the Operational Plans Division of the Air Staff, Plans, and no effort was made by either the Post War Division or the Air Staff, Intelligence, to provide the Post War Division with intelligence reports related to the postwar world.

On 28 July 1945 a letter sent from the Air Staff, Intelligence, to the Operational Plans Division of the Air Staff, Plans, concerning the rank of postwar United States military attachés was forwarded to the PWD.[14] Included in this letter was a brief intelligence estimate of the major states with whom the United States would have relations and to which it

14. 145.96–128 (III-M-B); 8090–32.

would send military attachés. The estimate concerning Russia is quoted in its entirety:

> Land mass army and air force presently of equal predominance. With the advent of peace concerted efforts will be directed toward complete development of air power. Country poses greatest threat to security of United States.[15]

This brief intelligence summary apparently had no effect on the PWD, for there is no evidence of any modification in its position that the Soviet danger only existed in the distant future. The consideration of enemies was not terribly important to the postwar planners except as a means of reinforcing its case for a large postwar Air Force; this may explain the lack of concern about an intelligence estimate at variance with the assumptions of the Division. The evidence is substantial that the Air Staff, Intelligence, perceived the postwar Soviet danger to be of some immediate concern. There is no indication, however, that the officers of the Air Staff, Intelligence, made any attempt to articulate either verbally or in writing to the postwar planners their concern about the intentions and capabilities of the Soviet Union.

The military's apparent distrust of the civilian intellectual raises two questions: Why was there such distrust, and what was its impact on policy? The distrust in the 1943–45 period was largely a result of the criticism that the intellectuals had directed against the military in the twenties and thirties, which blamed the military for the initiation of World War I and censured it for America's entry into that war. The intellectuals' fear of militarism, a fear that is difficult to substantiate, engendered a corresponding distrust of intellectuals by the military. The military intellectual was tolerated by the military leadership and in some cases—if his loyalties to the military profession exceeded his loyalties to the intellectual community—admired. The result of this mutual distrust was the absence of civilian intellectuals from the AAF postwar planning process.

The more important of these two questions is what relevance this military distrust of the intellectual will have on future military planning. If the intellectual is extremely critical of the military profession and constantly accuses it of undermining democracy, while the military not only maintains democratic values but is also a defender of democratic institutions, then a mistrust of the civilian intellectual will continue and his voice in the military planning process will be either distrusted or absent. If, however, the civilian intellectual is objective when he criticizes the military profession, and recognizes strengths as well as weaknesses, the rapport between the intellectual and the military man may be fruitful for both. If the military leadership looks for the kind of intellectual advice that can broaden its perspective, then the military planning process may avoid some of the deficiencies evident in this case study.

15. *Ibid.*, p. 2.

Part of getting the right answers is asking the right questions. The AAF planners often got the right answers to the questions they asked, but, by failing to ask the appropriate questions, they missed some of the important lessons of the war that might have been most useful to them. How is it possible for a military service to produce the kind of planners who will ask the kinds of questions that could challenge its doctrine? One solution might be to import into the planning process scholars who are neither committed to the service doctrine nor likely to accept any doctrine uncritically. Another possibility would be to have a number of competitive doctrines represented in the planning process so that inconsistencies and irrelevancies might be noted and corrected. Neither solution was utilized in the 1943–45 period; consequently, Air Corps doctrine was never questioned or debated by the postwar planners.

The AAF planners did an enormous amount of postwar planning in the 1943–45 period, considerably more than either the Army or the Navy did and considerably more than I anticipated when I undertook this study. This planning was done for the wrong reasons. The motivations that initiated the process and the motivations of the planners themselves were not based on trying to analyze postwar international relations in order to design an Air Force that would meet the dangers to United States national security which might result from the international situation. Instead, the planning was done to gain autonomy for the postwar Air Force, a goal that was essentially achieved before the planning process had begun.

To recognize that the planners planned for the wrong reasons is interesting but not very helpful if one is to try to learn from the experience. Of much greater interest is the answer to the question: If the parochial motivation in postwar planning had not existed, would the AAF leaders have initiated a planning process which at the end of the war would have provided the kind of alternatives incorporated in the various Air Force plans? No positive answer can be made to such a question, but the examples of the Army and the Navy give some insights. The Navy postwar planning was also parochially motivated, and the Navy did accomplish some detailed planning prior to V-J Day. The Army, with very little parochial motivation, did very little contingency planning. It can therefore tentatively be said that wartime planning for postwar contingencies would have been minimal without interservice rivalry.

Bureaucratic lethargy has not been greatly evident in the United States military in the past thirty years, primarily because of the keen interservice and intraservice competition which began in earnest in World War II and has continued to the present. The costs of this competition are sometimes high; its benefits, though not always as obvious as the costs, can also be considerable.

The Air Corps leaders had become aware of the political side of military decisions during the long twenty-year quest for autonomy. Only by seriously considering grand strategy and the political and military ends of warfare could the Air Corps make the kinds of assumptions that

could be used to prove their case for a separate Air Force.   The organization of the AAF in World War II was based on immediate operational
requirements, and the decisions that related to political considerations were
normally made within the War Department (either in the Strategy and
Policy Group of the Operations Division or by the Civil Affairs Division of
the War Department).[16]

With the establishment of the Special Projects Office and the Post
War Division in 1943, the Army Air Force was faced with a bureaucratic
dilemma.   Where were the long-range assumptions concerning American
foreign policy goals, potential adversaries, and utility of a future international organization to be formulated?   The State Department, the
Strategy and Policy Group of the OPD, the Civil Affairs Division of the
War Department, and the SPD, and the Army Air Corps and War Department intelligence staffs were logical sources for this kind of assumptive
information.   Although there is evidence that all of these sources made
at least a small contribution to the development of the postwar plans, the
PWD made assumptions and drew up plans based on these assumptions
without having made a rational attempt to draw upon these external
sources for guidance and without fully using the guidance they did
receive.   This can be explained by examining the mandate under which
the PWD operated.   General Kuter and Colonel Moffat understood the
primary purpose of this Division: the composition of plans that would
fully justify a large, autonomous postwar Air Force.

The content of these postwar plans highlights a number of fundamental errors made by the military planners, and these errors in turn
point up some of the real difficulties that face planners in large bureaucra-
cies.   The planners neither incorporated the lessons of World War II
into their plans nor even attempted to determine what these lessons might
be.   They failed to identify the Soviet Union as a short-term potential
enemy.   They selected 70 groups as the final bargaining figure for the
Air Force on an arbitrary basis.   In fact, what is most characteristic of all
the plans is the arbitrary nature of the recommended force levels.

What was the result of all this planning?   The final postwar
plan, the 70-group plan, became AAF policy by the late fall of 1945.   The
planners had succeeded in converting their plan into Air Force policy
because they were so closely in tune with AAF policy.   This is the
fundamental reason why the PWD was formed and left unburdened
by tasks unrelated to postwar planning, and why it was successful in
having the 70-group plan converted into AAF policy.   The PWD served
two policy goals: independence and a large postwar Air Force.   It
opened no new policy vistas, did no really creative planning, and it formed
assumptions to justify force levels in a very limited sense.

Can planners in the military (or, for that matter, in any large organization) look at the future in an objective manner, be creative in the plans

16. Interviews with Giffin and Kuter.   Interview with Colonel George Lincoln,
U.S. Army, 9 May 1966.

they formulate, and successfully convert the plan into policy ? This case study does not and cannot answer this question. It does show the difficulties of objective planning when the outputs of the planning process are determined by the policymakers before the planning begins.

Colonel Moffat and his staff entered into planning in what may be considered an inverse fashion. The end sought was not national security through a properly balanced military defensive and deterrent force but rather an autonomous, powerful United States Air Force which would be the first line of defense, the largest of the three military services, and the recipient of the largest share of the defense budget. Assumptions were drawn not as an initial step in the planning process, which would, in turn, provide the guidance for the structure, size, and deployment of the military forces. Instead, they were drawn in order to lead to the end desired. Thus, only the guidance of sources external to the Post War Division of the Air Staff, Plans, which contributed to that end was used by Colonel Moffat and his staff.

Bibliography

Unpublished Government Sources

Assistant Chief of Staff, Plans—Office File.
Assistant Chief of Staff, Plans—Daily Activity Reports.
Post War Division—Office File.
Special Projects Office—Office File.
Special Projects Office—Daily Activity Reports.

These files and reports are located in the Air Force Archives, Maxwell Air Force Base, Montgomery, Alabama. They contain both classified and unclassified materials.

Unpublished Private Sources

Arnold, Henry H. Manuscripts Division, Library of Congress.
Kuter, Laurence S. Special Collections Office, USAF Academy Library.

The author had access to both the classified and unclassified portions of these private papers.

Published Government Documents

Anderson, O. A. *A Study to Determine the Minimum Air Power the United States Should Have at the Conclusion of the War in Europe.* April 1943.
Command and Employment of Air Power. Field Manual 100–20. July 21, 1943.
The Public Papers and Addresses of Franklin D. Roosevelt. Compiled by Samuel I. Rosenman. *1939, War—and Neutrality. 1940, War—and Aid to Democracies. 1941, The Call to Battle Stations. 1942, Humanity on the Defensive. 1943, The Tide Turns. 1944–45, Victory and the Threshold of Peace.* New York: Harper, 1949–50.
Readings on the Functions of Military Air Power. Maxwell Air Force Base, Alabama: Documentary Research Division, Air University, 1957.
U.S. House of Representatives, Committee on Military Affairs. *Hearings on Demobilization.* 79th Cong., 2d sess., 1946.
———. *Hearings on Universal Military Training.* 79th Cong., 1st sess., 1945.

————. *Hearings on Universal Military Training.* 79th Cong., 2d sess., 1946.

U.S. House of Representatives, Joint Committee on Post-war Military Policy (Woodrum Committee). *Hearings on Proposal to Establish a Single Department of Armed Forces.* 78th Cong., 2d sess., 1944.

————. *Hearings on Universal Military Training.* 79th Cong., 1st sess., 1945.

U.S. House of Representatives. *Report on Post-war Military Policy.* Report No. 1645. 78th Cong., 2d sess., June 15, 1944.

U.S. House of Representatives. *Report on Universal Military Training.* Report No. 857. 79th Cong., 1st sess., July 15, 1945.

U.S. Senate, Committee on Military Affairs. *Hearings on Demobilization of Armed Forces.* 79th Cong., 1st sess., 1945.

————. *Hearings on Demobilization of Armed Forces.* 79th Cong., 2d sess., 1946.

————. *Hearings on Department of Armed Forces, Department of Military Security.* 79th Cong., 1st sess., 1945.

————. *Hearings on S.84 and S.1482, Unification of Armed Forces.* 79th Cong., 1st sess., 1945.

Official Histories

Boylan, Bernard. *Development of the Long-Range Escort Fighter.* Maxwell Air Force Base, Alabama: USAF Historical Study No. 136, 1955.

Butler, J. R. M. (ed.). *History of the Second World War: United Kingdom Military Series: Grand Strategy.* Vols. II, III, V, VI. London: Her Majesty's Stationery Office, 1956–64.

Cline, Ray S. *Washington Command Post: The Operations Division, United States Army in World War II: The War Department.* Washington: Office of the Chief of Military History, Department of the Army, 1951.

Craven, Wesley F., and Cate, James L. (eds.). *The Army Air Forces in World War II.* Vol. I, *Plans and Early Operations, January 1939 to August 1942.* Vol. II, *Europe: Torch to Point Blank, August 1942 to December 1943.* Vol. III, *Europe: Argument to V.E. Day, January 1944 to May 1945.* Vol. IV, *The Pacific: Guadalcanal to Saipan, August 1942 to July 1944.* Vol. V, *The Pacific: Matterhorn to Nagasaki, June 1944 to August 1945.* Vol. VI, *Men and Planes.* Chicago: University of Chicago Press, 1948–55.

Finney, Robert T. *History of the Air Corps Tactical School, 1920–1940.* Maxwell Air Force Base, Alabama: USAF Historical Study No. 100, 1955.

Glines, Carroll V. *The Compact History of the United States Air Force.* New York: Hawthorn Books, 1963.

Goldberg, Alfred (ed.). *A History of the United States Air Force, 1907–1957.* Princeton: Van Nostrand, 1957.

Grant, C. L. *AAF Air Defense Activities in the Mediterranean: 1942–1944.* Maxwell Air Force Base, Alabama: USAF Historical Study No. 66, 1954.

Greenfield, Kent Roberts (ed.). *Command Decisions.* New York: Harcourt, Brace, 1959.

Greer, Thomas H. *The Development of Air Doctrine in the Army Air Arm, 1917–1941.* Maxwell Air Force Base, Alabama: USAF Historical Study No. 89, 1955.

Holley, I. B. *Evolution of the Liaison-Type Airplane: 1917–1944.* Washington: AAF Historical Study No. 44, 1946.

Matloff, Maurice. *Strategic Planning for Coalition Warfare: 1943–1944; United States Army in World War II: The War Department.* Washington: Office of the Chief of Military History, Department of the Army, 1959.

McClendon, R. Earl. *Autonomy of the Air Arm.* Maxwell Air Force Base, Alabama: Air University Documentary Research Study, 1954.

Mooney, Chase C. *Organization of Military Aeronautics, 1935–1945.* Washington: AAF Historical Study No. 46, 1946.

Pogue, Forrest C. *The Supreme Command: United States Army in World War II: The European Theater of Operations.* Washington: Office of the Chief of Military History, Department of the Army, 1954.

Saunders, Chauncey E. *Demobilization Planning for the United States Air Force.* Maxwell Air Force Base, Alabama: USAF Historical Study No. 59, 1954.

The War Reports of General of the Army George C. Marshall, General of the Army H. H. Arnold, Fleet Admiral Ernest J. King. New York: Lippincott, 1947.

Watson, Mark Skinner. *Chief of Staff: Prewar Plans and Preparations, United States Army in World War II: The War Department.* Historical Division, Department of the Army, 1950.

Williams, Edwin L. *Legislative History of the AAF and USAF, 1941–1951.* Maxwell Air Force Base, Alabama: USAF Historical Study No. 84, 1955.

Memoirs and Biographies

Arnold, Henry H. *Global Misson.* New York: Harper, 1949.

Bryant, Arthur. *Triumph in the West.* Garden City, N.Y.: Doubleday, 1959.

Churchill, Winston S. *The Second World War.* 6 vols. Boston: Houghton Mifflin Company, 1948–53.

Dean, John R. *The Strange Alliance: The Story of Our Efforts at Wartime Cooperation with Russia.* New York: Viking, 1947.

Eisenhower, Dwight D. *Crusade in Europe.* Garden City, N.Y.: Doubleday, 1948.

Forrestal, James V. *The Forrestal Dairies.* Edited by Walter Millis with E. S. Duffield. New York: Viking, 1951.

Groves, Leslie R. *Now It Can Be Told: The Story of the Manhattan Project*. New York: Harper, 1962.

Hartz, Robert (ed.). *Way of a Fighter: The Memoirs of Claire Lee Chennault*. New York: Putnam, 1948.

Hurley, Alfred Francis. *Billy Mitchell: Crusader for Air Power*. New York: Franklin Watts, 1964.

Kuter, Laurence S. *Airman at Yalta*. New York: Duell, 1955.

Leahy, William D. *I Was There*. New York: Whittlesey House, Mc-Graw, 1950.

Levine, Isaac Don. *Mitchell: Pioneer of Air Power*. New York: Duell, 1943.

Payne, Robert. *The Marshall Story: A Biography of General George C. Marshall*. New York: Prentice-Hall, 1951.

Pogue, Forrest C. *George C. Marshall: Education of a General, 1880–1939*. New York: Viking, 1963.

———. *George C. Marshall: Ordeal and Hope, 1939–1942*. New York: Viking, 1966.

Sherwood, Robert Emmett. *Roosevelt and Hopkins: An Intimate History*. New York: Harper, 1950.

Stimson, Henry L., and Bundy, McGeorge. *On Active Service in Peace and War*. New York: Harper, 1947.

Truman, Harry S. *Memoirs*. 2 vols. Garden City, N.Y.: Doubleday, 1956.

Wedemeyer, Albert C. *Wedemeyer Reports*. New York: Henry Holt, 1958.

Secondary Works

Arnold, Henry H., and Eaker, Ira C. *Winged Warfare*. New York: Harper, 1941.

Aron, Raymond. *The Century of Total War*. Boston: Beacon Press, 1955.

Bond, Douglas D. *The Love and Fear of Flying*. New York: International Universities Press, 1952.

Brodie, Bernard. *Strategy in the Missile Age*. Princeton: Princeton University Press, 1959.

Caidin, Martin. *Black Thursday*. New York: E. P. Dutton, 1960.

Davis, Vincent. *Postwar Defense Policy and the U.S. Navy, 1943–1946*. Chapel Hill: University of North Carolina Press, 1966.

de Seversky, Alexander P. *Victory Through Air Power*. New York: Simon and Schuster, 1942.

Douhet, Giulio. *The Command of the Air*. Translated by Sheila Fischer. Rome: Rivista Aeronautica, 1958.

Dupre, Flint O. (ed.). *U.S. Air Force Biographical Dictionary*. New York: Franklin Watts, 1965.

Earle, Edward Mead (ed.). *Makers of Modern Strategy: Military Thought from Machiavelli to Hitler*. Princeton: Princeton University Press, 1952.

Ekirch, Arthur A., Jr. *The Civilian and the Military*. New York: Oxford University Press, 1956.

Emme, Eugene M. (ed.). *The Impact of Air Power*. Princeton: Van Nostrand, 1959.

F. D. R.: His Personal Letters, 1928–1945. Vol II. Edited by Elliott Roosevelt. New York: Duell, 1950.

Feis, Herbert. *Churchill—Roosevelt—Stalin*. Princeton: Princeton University Press, 1957.

Fox, William T. R. *The Superpowers: The United States, Britain, and the Soviet Union—Their Responsibility for Peace*. New York: Harper, 1944.

Gilpin, Robert, and Wright, Christopher. *Scientists and National Policy-Making*. New York: Columbia University Press, 1964.

Greenfield, Kent Roberts. *American Strategy in World War II: A Reconsideration*. Baltimore: Johns Hopkins Press, 1963.

Hammond, Paul Y. *Organizing for Defense: The American Military Establishment in the Twentieth Century*. Princeton: Princeton University Press, 1961.

Holley, I. B. *Ideas and Weapons*. New Haven: Yale University Press, 1953.

Huntington, Samuel P. *The Common Defense: Strategic Programs in National Politics*. New York: Columbia University Press, 1961.

———. *The Soldier and the State: The Theory and Politics of Civil-Military Relations*. Cambridge: Harvard University Press, 1959.

Janowitz, Morris. *The Professional Soldier: A Social and Political Portrait*. Glencoe, Ill.: Free Press, 1960.

Kissinger, Henry A. *The Necessity for Choice: Prospects of American Foreign Policy*. New York: Harper, 1960.

——— (ed.). *Problems of National Strategy: A Book of Readings*. New York: Praeger, 1965.

Kolodziej, Edward A. *The Uncommon Defense and Congress, 1945–1963*. Columbus: Ohio State University Press, 1966.

Mahan, Alfred Thayer. *The Influence of Sea Power Upon History, 1660–1783*. Boston: Little, Brown, 1918.

Masland, John W., and Radway, Laurence I. *Soldiers and Scholars: Military Education and National Policy*. Princeton: Princeton University Press, 1957.

Millis, Walter (ed.). *American Military Thought*. Indianapolis: Bobbs-Merrill, 1966.

———. *Arms and Men: A Study in American Military History*. New York: G. P. Putnam, 1956.

———, with Mansfield, Harvey C., and Stein, Harold. *Arms and the State: Civil-Military Elements in National Policy*. New York: Twentieth Century Fund, 1958.

Nelson, Otto L., Jr. *National Security and the General Staff*. Washington: Infantry Journal Press, 1946.

121

Quester, George H. *Deterrence before Hiroshima: The Airpower Background of Modern Strategy.* New York: Wiley, 1966.

Register of Graduates and Former Cadets of the United States Military Academy. West Point, N.Y.: West Point Alumni Foundation, Inc., 1965.

Ries, John C. *The Management of Defense: Organization and Control of the U.S. Armed Services.* Baltimore: Johns Hopkins Press, 1964.

Schelling, Thomas C. *The Strategy of Conflict.* New York: Oxford University Press, 1963.

Schilling, Warner R., Hammond, Paul Y., and Snyder, Glenn H. *Strategy, Politics, and Defense Budgets.* New York: Columbia University Press, 1962.

Sherman, William C. *Air Warfare.* New York: Ronald Press, 1926.

Sprout, Harold, and Sprout, Margaret. *Toward a New Order of Sea Power: American Naval Policy and the World Scene, 1918–1922.* Princeton: Princeton University Press, 1940.

Stein, Harold. *American Civil-Military Decisions: A Book of Case Studies.* Tuscaloosa: University of Alabama Press for the Twentieth Century Fund, 1963.

Weigley, Russell F. *Towards an American Army: Military Thought from Washington to Marshall.* New York: Columbia University Press, 1962.

Who's Who in Aviation: A Directory of Living Men and Women Who Have Contributed to the Growth of Aviation in the United States, 1942–1943. New York: Ziff-Davis, 1942.

Who's Who in World Aviation, Vol I. Washington: American Aviation Publications, 1955.

Wilmot, Chester. *The Struggle for Europe.* New York: Harper, 1952.

Wohlstetter, Roberta. *Pearl Harbor: Warning and Decision.* Stanford: Stanford University Press, 1962.

Articles and Periodicals

Aerospace Historian (Airpower Historian), 1954–66.

Air University Review (Air University Quarterly Review), 1947–66.

Arnold, Henry H. "Air Strategy for Victory," *Military Review* (October 1943).

———. "Isolation of the Battlefield by Air Power," *Military Review* (July 1944).

Birdsall, Stephen P. "The Destroyer Escorts," *Airpower Historian* (July 1965).

Bowman, Richard C. "Organizational Fanaticism: A Case Study of Allied Air Operations against the U-Boat during World War II," *Airpower Historian* (April 1963).

Driscoll, John J. "Impact of Weapons Technology on Air Warfare, 1941–1945," *Airpower Historian* (January 1959).

Edmunds, Kinzie B. "Lessons from World War II," *Military Review* (June 1941).

Fairchild, Muir S. "Traditionalism Is a Deadly Danger," *Airpower Historian* (April 1958).

Flying Safety, 1954–66.

Fox, William T. R. "Civilians, Soldiers, and American Military Policy," *World Politics* (April 1955).

Greene, Fred. "The Military View of American National Policy," *American Historical Review* (January 1961).

Holloway, Bruce K. "High Sub-Sonic Speeds for Air Warfare," *Air University Quarterly Review* (Fall 1947).

Military Review, 1940–46.

New York Times, 1943–45.

Olson, Mancur, Jr. "The Economics of Strategic Bombing in World War II," *Airpower Historian* (April 1962).

Smith, Dale O. "One Way Combat," *Air University Quarterly Review* (Fall 1947).

Spaatz, Carl. "If We Should Have to Fight Again," *Life*, July 5 and August 16, 1948.

Taylor, Joe Gray. "They Taught Tactics," *Aerospace Historian* (Summer 1966).

"Universal Military Training and National Security," American Academy of Political and Social Science, *Annals* (September 1945).

Zeller, Anchara F. "Psychological Factors in Escape," United States Air Force Study, 1949.

Lectures

Emerson, William R. "Operation Pointblank: A Tale of Bombers and Fighters." United States Air Force Academy, Harmon Memorial Lectures in Military History, No. 4, 1962.

Hansell, H. S. "The Development of the U.S. Concept of Bombardment Operations." Lecture delivered at the Air War College, Maxwell Air Force Base, Alabama, November 12, 1953.

———. "Strategic Air Warfare." Talk given to the officers at Loring Air Force Base, Maine, 1966. (Exact date unknown.)

Healey, Denis. Lecture given at Columbia University, March 24, 1964.

Kuter, Laurence S. "American Air Power—School Theories vs. World War Facts." Lecture delivered at the Air Corps Tactical School, 1938.

———. "Organization of Top Echelons in World War II." Lecture delivered at the Air War College, Maxwell Air Force Base, Alabama, February 29, 1949.

Lincoln, George A. "Postwar Planning." Lecture delivered at the Air War College, Maxwell Air Force Base, Alabama, November 3, 1947.

Tompkins, William F. "War Time Planning for Demobilization." Lecture delivered at the Army War College, Carlisle Barracks, Pa., December 20, 1950.

Other Unpublished Material

Flugel, Raymond R.   "United States Air Power Doctrine: A Study of the Influence of William Mitchell and Giulio Douhet at the Air Corps Tactical School, 1921–1935." Ph.D. diss., University of Oklahoma, 1965.

Legere, Lawrence J., Jr.   "Unification of the Armed Forces."   Ph.D. diss., Harvard University, 1950.

Posvar, Wesley W.   "Strategy Expertise and National Security." Ph.D. diss., Harvard University, 1964.

Schilling, Warner R.   "Admirals and Foreign Policy, 1913–1919." Ph.D. diss., Yale University, 1954.

Wilson, Donald.   "Origin of a Theory for Air Strategy."   Private study, 1962 (typewritten).

Interviews

The inability to interview such key men as General Arnold and Colonel Moffat was a considerable limitation, but the following individuals gave invaluable information in the areas of research where official records and secondary sources proved inadequate.

Major General Frederick L. Anderson, USAF, Ret.
Brigadier General William W. Bessell, Jr., USA, Ret.
General Charles P. Cabell, USAF, Ret.
Lieutenant General John W. Carpenter, III, USAF
Brigadier General F. Trubee Davison, USAF, Ret.
Lieutenant General Fred M. Dean, USAF
Alexander P. de Seversky
Lieutenant General Ira C. Eaker, USAF, Ret.
Lieutenant General Harold L. George, USAF, Ret.
Brigadier General Sidney F. Giffin, USAF, Ret.
Lieutenant General Barney M. Giles, USAF, Ret.
Major General Pierpont Morgan Hamilton, USAF, Ret.
Major General Haywood S. Hansell, USAF, Ret.
Major General Norris B. Harbold, USAF, Ret.
Brigadier General Glen C. Jamison, USAF, Ret.
General Laurence S. Kuter, USAF, Ret.
Colonel George A. Lincoln, USA
Philip E. Mosley
General Lauris Norstad, USAF, Ret.
Brigadier General Noel F. Parish, USAF, Ret.
Guido Perera
General Jacob E. Smart, USAF, Ret.
General Frederick H. Smith, Jr., USAF, Ret.
Lieutenant General Walter E. Todd, USAF, Ret.
Major General William F. Tompkins, USA, Ret.
Major General Donald Wilson, USAF, Ret.

Glossary

AAA	Anti-Aircraft Artillery
AAF	Army Air Force
AC/AS, Plans	Assistant Chief of Air Staff, Plans
ACTS	Air Corps Tactical School
AGF	Army Ground Forces
ASF	Army Service Forces
AWPD	Air War Plans Division
AWPD/1	The first plan composed by Air War Plans Division (August 1941)
CCS	Combined Chiefs of Staff
FM	Field Manual
Frantic	Code name for shuttle bombing missions to and from the Soviet Union
G-3	Operations and Training Division of the War Department
GHQ	General Headquarters
HB	Heavy Bomber
IPF	International Police Force
IPWAF	Initial Post War Air Force (the 105-group plan)
JCS	Joint Chiefs of Staff
JPS	Joint Staff Planners
JSSC	Joint Strategic Survey Committee
M/LB	Medium or Light Bomber
OC&R	Operations, Commitments, and Requirements (AC/AS-3)
OPD	Operations Division (War Department)
PWAF plan number 2	Post War Air Force plan number 2 (the 75-group plan)
PWD	Post War Division
RAF	Royal Air Force
R&R	Routing and Record Sheet (similar to a memorandum)
SPD	Special Planning Division (War Department Special Staff)
SPO	Special Projects Office (Headquarters, Army Air Force)
TC	Troop Carrier
T/O	Table of Organization

T/O&E	Table of Organization and Equipment
USSBS	United States Strategic Bombing Survey
VHB	Very Heavy Bomber
V-J plan	AAF demobilization plan for the period following the defeat of Japan
VLR	Very Long Range
WDSBO	War Department Special Budget Office
WDSS	War Department Special Staff

Index